TWAYNE'S WORLD AUTHORS SERIES
A Survey of the World's Literature

DENMARK

Leif Sjoberg, State University of New York at Stony Brook
EDITOR

Henrik Pontoppidan

TWAS 524

HENRIK PONTOPPIDAN

By P. M. Mitchell
University of Illinois at Urbana

TWAYNE PUBLISHERS
A DIVISION OF G. K. HALL & CO., BOSTON

Copyright © 1979 by G. K. Hall & Co.

Published in 1979 by Twayne Publishers,
A Division of G. K. Hall & Co.
All Rights Reserved

Printed on permanent/durable acid-free paper and bound
in the United States of America

First Printing

Frontispiece sketch of Henrik
Pontoppidan by P. S. Krøyer

Library of Congress Cataloging in Publication Data

Mitchell, Phillip Marshall, 1916–
Henrik Pontoppidan.

(Twayne's world authors series ; TWAS 524 : Denmark)
Bibliography: pp. 149–55
Includes Index.
1. Pontoppidan, Henrik, 1857–1943.
2. Authors, Danish—19th century—Biography.
3. Authors, Danish—20th century—Biography.
PT8175.P6Z728   839.8′1′36 [B]   78-21609
ISBN 0–8057–6366–X

Contents

About the Author
Preface
Chronology

1.	Wellsprings	13
2.	Impressions into Words	25
3.	Iconoclastic Pastoral	35
4.	Essays in Morality	39
5.	Political Parables	46
6.	Patriotic Interludes	54
7.	The Kingdom Comes Not	61
8.	Memoir and Pathos	76
9.	Will and Testament	83
10.	Case Histories	107
11.	Reassessment	115
12.	A Capstone	125
13.	Reflections	130
14.	Conclusion	137
	Notes and References	145
	Selected Bibliography	149
	Index	156

About the Author

P. M. Mitchell received the Ph.D. degree from the University of Illinois in 1942. He has been a professor in the Department of Germanic Languages at the University of Illinois since 1958. He has taught previously at Cornell University, Harvard University, and the University of Kansas. He has been a guest professor at the University of Wisconsin and the University of Aarhus.

Professor Mitchell's publications include: *A Bibliographical Guide to Danish Literature* (1951); *Selected Essays of Ludvig Holberg*, translated, with an Introduction and Notes (1955); *A History of Danish Literature*, with an introductory chapter by Mogens Haugsted (New York, 1958, 2nd, augmented edition, 1971); *A Bibliography of English Imprints of Denmark* (1960); Vilhelm Grønbech, *Religious Currents in the Nineteenth Century*, translated from the Danish (with W. D. Paden) (1964); *A Bibliography of 17th Century German Imprints of Denmark and the Duchies of Schleswig-Holstein* I–II (1969); III (1976); *Vilhelm Grønbech. En Indføring* (1970); *Anthology of Danish Literature*, bilingual edition, edited with F. J. Billeskov Jansen (1971); *Bibliography of Modern Icelandic Literature in Translation* (with Kenneth H. Ober) (1975); *The Royal Guest and Other Classical Danish Narrative*, edited and translated (with Kenneth H. Ober) (1977); *Vilhelm Grønbech* (TWAS 1978); *Halldór Hermannsson* (1978).

Professor Mitchell has served as co-editor of the *Journal of English and Germanic Philology* since 1959.

Preface

Few writers are better established in Danish literature than Henrik Pontoppidan. Several of his works have appeared in many editions and are still being read today in Denmark. No syllabus of Danish literature for schools is conceivable without at least some of his short stories. He is distinguished by his long career as a writer—his first book was published in 1881, his last, in 1943—and particularly by the fact that he shared the Nobel Prize for literature in 1917.

Just as the number of revisions Pontoppidan undertook on his many works make it practically impossible for the interested reader or scholar to examine and compare all versions, so too the number of critical articles published about Pontoppidan as a writer seems insuperable, even disregarding the myriad of book reviews that have appeared in Danish newspapers and periodicals. Every critic or literary historian who has dealt with Danish literature had something to say at some time about Pontoppidan. Consequently, every aesthetic and political persuasion is represented among his critics. A collective evaluation of the response to Pontoppidan's books would be a difficult task were it to be all-inclusive. The standard bibliography of Danish literature between 1900 and 1950 (*Dansk skønlitterært forfatterleksikon*, III, 1964) lists well over 300 articles about Pontoppidan, as well as a small number of monographs published by about 1960. The statistics attest the insistence with which Pontoppidan's works have insinuated themselves into the thought and lives of educated and articulate Danes.

Chronology

1857 Henrik Pontoppidan born in Fredericia, Denmark, July 24.
1863 Pontoppidan's father accepts a call to Randers.
1873 Pontoppidan completes secondary schooling in Randers; goes to Copenhagen to study at the Polytechnical Institute.
1877 Successfully completes Part I of his studies in engineering.
1879 Withdraws from the Polytechnical Institute; teaches (until 1882) at his brother Morten's folk-high-school, first in Frerslev, then in Hjørlunde, on the island of Zealand.
1880 Serves one summer with Danish army, corps of engineers.
1881 Makes his literary debut with the story "Et Endeligt" ("The End of a Life") in the journal *Ude og Hjemme* (Sept.); publishes a collection of short stories, *Stækkede Vinger* (*Clipped Wings*); and marries Mette Marie Hansen (Dec.).
1883 Publishes *Sandinge Menighed* (*Sandinge Parish*) a novel, and *Landsbybilleder* (*Village Sketches*), a collection of short stories.
1885 *Ung Elskov* (*Young Love*), short novel.
1886 *Mimoser* (*Mimosas*), short novel.
1887 *Fra Hytterne* (*From the Huts*), short stories; *Isbjørnen* (*The Polar Bear*), short novel; contributes (until 1889) to Copenhagen daily *Politiken*.
1888 *Spøgelser* (*Ghosts*), short novel.
1890 *Skyer* (*Clouds*), short stories; *Reisebilder aus Dänemark*, travel guide (in German); *Natur* (*Nature*), two novellas; *Krøniker* (*Chronicles*), parables.
1891 *Muld* (*Sod*), first volume of the trilogy *Det forjættede Land*; contributes to Copenhagen daily *Kjøbenhavns Børstidende*.
1892 *Det forjættede Land* (*The Promised Land*), second volume of the trilogy by that title; Pontoppidan divorced; marries Antoinette C. E. Kofoed.
1893 *Minder* (*Memories*), short novel.

1894 *Nattevagt* (*Night Watch*), *Den gamle Adam* (*The Old Adam*), both short novels.
1895 *Dommens Dag* (*Judgment Day*), third volume of the trilogy *Det forjættede Land*.
1896 *Højsang* (*Hymn*), short novel.
1898 *Lykke-Per, hans Ungdom* (*Lykke-Per, His Youth*) and *Lykke-Per finder Skatten* (*Lykke-Per Finds the Treasure*), volumes I and II of *Lykke-Per*.
1899 *Lykke-Per, hans Kærlighed* (*Lykke-Per, His Love*) and *Lykke-Per i det Fremmede* (*Lykke-Per Abroad*).
1900 *Lille Rødhætte* (*Little Red Riding Hood*), *Det ideale Hjem* (*The Ideal Home*), both short novels.
1901 *Lykke-Per, hans store Værk* (*Lykke-Per, His Great Work*).
1902 *De vilde Fugle* (*The Wild Birds*), a dramatization of *Højsang*; *Lykke-Per og hans Kæreste* (*Lykke-Per and his Fiancée*).
1903 *Lykke-Per, hans Rejse til Amerika* (*Lykke-Per, His Journey to America*).
1904 *Lykke-Per, hans sidste Kamp* (*Lykke-Per, His Last Battle*), concluding volume of *Lykke-Per*.
1905 *Lykke-Per* rewritten in three volumes; *Borgmester Hoeck og hans Hustru* (*Mayor Hoeck and His Wife*), short novel.
1906 *Asgaardrejen* (*The Wild Huntsman*), play.
1907 *Det store Spøgelse* (*The Great Apparition*), novella; *Hans Kvast og Melusine* (*Merry Andrew and Melusina*), short novel.
1908 *Den kongelige Gæst* (*The Royal Guest*), short novel.
1912 *Torben og Jytte* (*Torben and Jytta*), volume I of *De Dødes Rige* (*The Realm of the Dead*).
1913 *Storeholt*, volume II of *De Dødes Rige*.
1914 *Toldere og Syndere* (*Publicans and Sinners*), volume III of *De Dødes Rige*; *Thora van Deken*, a dramatization of *Lille Rødhætte*; *Kirken og dens Mænd* (*The Church and its Men*).
1915 *Enslevs Død* (*Enslev's Death*), volume IV of *De Dødes Rige*.
1916 *Favsingholm*, concluding volume of *De Dødes Rige*.
1917 Pontoppidan shares Nobel Prize for Literature with Karl Gjellerup (1857–1919).

Chronology

1918 *Lykke-Per* rewritten in two volumes; *Et Kærlighedseventyr (A Love Story)*, short novel.
1920 *En Vinterrejse (A Winter Journey)*, travel book.
1927 *Mands Himmerig (Man's Heaven)*, novel.
1933 *Drengeaar (Boyhood Years)*, memoirs.
1936 *Hamskifte (Sloughing)*, memoirs.
1938 *Arv og Gæld (Inheritance and Debt)*, memoirs.
1940 *Familieliv (Family Life)*, memoirs.
1943 *Undervejs til mig selv (Underway to myself)*, a revision of the first four volumes of memoirs; Pontoppidan dies in Charlottenlund, a suburb of Copenhagen, August 21.

CHAPTER 1

Wellsprings

I Domestic Circumstances

BY striking coincidence, Henrik Pontoppidan was born the same year, 1857, as two other Danish writers who were to achieve international stature: Herman Bang (d. 1912), the most original practitioner of a naturalistic technique at the turn of the century, and Karl Gjellerup (d. 1919), who came to write in German as well as in Danish and who shared the Nobel Prize for literature with Pontoppidan in 1917. Pontoppidan and Bang have maintained their eminent positions in Danish literature and their books continue to be published and read. Gjellerup is now little more than a name. If Herman Bang remains unexcelled as a technician in the art of narration, Pontoppidan remains unexcelled as a chronicler of his own time as well as a narrator of philosophical and psychological bent whose best works stand up under repeated reading and critical scrutiny.

Blessed with a name that makes all but the classical scholar outside Denmark stumble, Pontoppidan is by virtue of that name associated with a conservative Danish cultural heritage. In the mid-nineteenth century, when Henrik Pontoppidan was born in the medium-sized Jutland town of Fredericia, the Lutheran clergy was still a force in Danish society. Lives were guided by the admonitions of the state church, and the name Pontoppidan was as closely identified with Danish Lutheranism as any name in the country. In his autobiography, Pontoppidan mentions the fact that by the mid-eighteenth century there were 300 Danish clergymen who had borne the clumsy name Pontoppidan, which originated from the seventeenth-century translation of the Danish place name "Broby" ("bridge city") into the Latin, *pons oppidanus*. He suggests that it was some-

13

thing of a burden to be born a Pontoppidan. The name was not one to be overlooked and in Denmark the ecclesiastical association was inescapable. No wonder that some latter-day Pontopiddans have translated their names back to Broby. No wonder either that so many of the characters in Pontoppidan's books are clergymen. And no wonder that Pontoppidan's clergymen are not his heroes.

Shortly after Pontoppidan's birth, his father, the Reverend Dines Pontoppidan, was transferred to the east Jutland city of Randers. Here Henrik spent his boyhood, the least disposed of sixteen children to carry on the puritanically Protestant cultural tradition which was his spiritual inheritance.

The young Henrik's gifts and interests seemed to lie in the fields of mathematics and technology. Through the encouragement of his mathematics teacher in Randers, he was permitted to go to Copenhagen at the early age of sixteen after finishing secondary school, to take an additional examination to enter the Polytechnical Institute (College of Engineering) in the Danish capital. He was among the fortunate who passed the examination and was admitted. He now plunged into a daily life very different from what he had known at home. For several years he devoted himself to the study of logarithmic tables, as he himself remarked metaphorically. The year 1876 brought both a youthful disappointment and a critical youthful experience: his hopes of being selected to accompany an expedition to Greenland were dashed, but a tiny inheritance from his grandfather enabled him to take a trip to the Swiss Alps. The sojourn in Switzerland was in several ways the beginning of a new life. It occupies a central position in the volume of his memoirs that bears the symbolic title *Hamskifte* (*Sloughing*). The experiences in the Swiss mountains were invigorating and inspiring to the young man and imbued him with a desire to travel more. He also had a brief, naive, and innocent interest in an Alpine maiden while he was there.

When he was once more in Denmark, his interests expanded. He read more widely and patronized the theater. Buoyed by his experiences abroad, he even attempted to become a playwright, understandably without success but nevertheless heading down a new path. He became progressively more disenchanted with the study of engineering and finally made the bold decision to become a writer. He withdrew from the Polytechnical Institute in 1877 without having any practical alternative with which to support himself. But one of his brothers had recently established a "folk-high-school," that peculiar Danish institution inspired by N. F. S. Grundtvig (1783–1872) which combined the ideals of popular enlightenment with those of adult education, and Henrik obtained a position as a teacher of practical subjects at the school. This arrangement gave him the time to write and read and the opportunity to broaden his acquaintance with his countrymen in general and country folk in particular.

Growing aware of the new currents to which Danish literature was subjected and which emanated to a large extent from the Danish critic Georg Brandes (1842–1927), Pontoppidan became an active member of the generation that subscribed to Brandes's dictum that literature should make social problems a matter of debate. Pontoppidan now read extensively in philosophical and literary treatises as well as Danish and foreign imaginative works. He addressed himself both to Søren Kierkegaard and the more recent Danish philosopher Harold Høffding (1843–1931), and to various French and German writers, notably Friedrich Nietzsche; he read Dostoevsky and other Russian novelists. He became acquainted with some of the leading young figures in Danish literature, Holger Drachmann (1846–1908) and Sophus Schandorph (1836–1901), and the Norwegian novelists Erik (1847–1923) and Amalie Skram (1847–1905), before making his own literary debut.

With the honorarium that he received for his first book, a volume of short stories, and with a publisher's advance, he cut himself loose from the somewhat restrictive atmosphere of the folk-high-school and married the country girl with whom he had fallen in love while there. Thus for a second time within a few years he made the same bold and radical decision: to write. After giving up his studies at the Polytechnical Institute, Pontoppidan had willfully put himself at a distance from Copenhagen, and after his marriage he and his wife lived several places in rural Zealand. He wrote vigorously and prolifically: stories, novels, and newspaper articles. As a journalist he entered the magic circle associated with Georg Brandes. Between 1881 and 1891 he had no fewer than a dozen books published. Some were short, to be sure, but taken together they indicate an unusually large and active production. Pontoppidan gained sufficient recognition that by 1890 he was asked to write a book about Denmark in German for the Danish Tourist Association. Though the book is an anomaly in his corpus, the request indicated that he was an established Danish writer who spoke authoritatively for his countrymen.

One need not know much of Pontoppidan's biography to realize that there must have been a shift from rural to urban life for him in mid-career. The many short stories about country life and journalistic sketches characteristically signed "Rusticus" give way to depictions of life in the capital and sketches signed with a new, telling pseudonym: "Urbanus." To be sure, Pontoppidan continued to depict the Danish landscape, but as Edvard Brandes (1847–1931) pointed out early in Pontoppidan's career, the landscape tends to be an idealized one; it is not really cartographic. The disharmony between life in the country and life in the city became a recurrent motif in Pontoppidan's works. Pontoppidan's three later multi-volume works make use of it in one way or another.

While the landscape may be idealized, it is treated with a spirit of synthesis and not of blind admiration. Pontoppidan by no means naively extols the virtue of rural living or portrays a joyous carefree existence in a peasant community. On the contrary, country life is strenuous and demanding. It takes its toll in sweat and tears. There is nothing about it suggestive of the spirit of Rousseau, though it is honest and satisfying.

It is of some interest to note that Henrik Pontoppidan was not the only one of the children of the Reverend Dines Pontoppidan to distinguish himself in Danish society. One of his older brothers, Morten, not only became a well-known clergyman and educator but also a widely read editor and writer (of among many other works a history of the United States), albeit not of imaginative literature. Another brother, Knud, became one of the leading figures in Danish medicine as a pioneer in both contemporary psychiatry and forensic medicine. Several of their sisters contracted marriages with men who came to play a role in the cultural and spiritual life of the nation, principally as clergymen. The experiences of his brothers and sisters suggest that Henrik was not really exceptional within his family, although the direction of development and the nature of Henrik's intellect were different from those of his brothers and sisters, with whom he shared a heritage. One might say that the many children were about equally gifted and that it was a matter of personality, in part shaped by early experiences, that made their goals and consequently their achievements different.

Had Henrik Pontoppidan lived a generation earlier, he might very well have chosen the cloth. Generation after generation of the Pontoppidan family had produced clergymen. It was almost to be expected that Pontoppidan sons at least considered entering the church and that Pontoppidan daughters were fated to wed clergymen. Nor was the Pontoppidan family unique in Danish society. There were other families with similar clerical traditions through the generations until the twentieth century when, as with the Pontoppidans, the demand of a clerical life diminished at the same time that the established church underwent a diminution of strength and influence. No family was more closely identified with the Danish Lutheran Church than the Pontoppidans, however. The very name has for generations suggested to most Danes one of two eighteenth-century bishops both named Erik Pontoppidan. One of them wrote a multitude of works in both Danish and German, including a lengthy expository catechism as well as a new hymn-book no Dane could easily escape. His name and works are not forgotten even today, although perhaps no longer so much on account of his religious writing as for his contribution to topography. Henrik Pontoppidan's own father Dines Pontoppidan had also written several books, the first of which, from the year 1841, unlike his later, religious works, described a trip to South America that he had undertaken as a marine chaplain early in his career.

It was of course not merely the name which made spiritual activity and social importance likely for succeeding generations of Pontoppidans, but rather the stratified nature of Danish society. There was much intermarriage between the children of clergymen and civil servants; considering that the church was a state church, one might say, between two groups of civil servants. Civil servants including clergy constituted a fairly closely interwoven group with common interests and similar backgrounds. They were not particularly well-to-do but neither did they have to struggle with poverty or uncertainty about tomorrow's meal or the wherewithal for one's old age. There were connections with landowners and well-established businessmen, but few close bonds with the tillers of the soil, the landed nobility, or the representatives of a rising international capitalism in Copenhagen. In short, the stratum of society from which Henrik Pontoppidan sprang had good reason to be satisfied with the status quo and to be politically conservative in its outlook.

II *Literary Circumstances*

How well-read a modern writer is in contemporary literature may remain indeterminate, but consciously or subconsciously he must have some general models in mind when he starts writing. Moreover, he is in part a child of his time: the mode of writing and the selection of subject matter is to some degree at least dictated by contemporary currents of thought and by contemporary needs and interests. And with regard to form and technique the writer is not an autodidact. He is also dependent on literary tradition and the literary climate it produces. The position of imaginative literature varies both from society to society and over time. Pontoppidan and his contemporaries were fortunate in being born into a highly literate society where belles-lettres enjoyed both respect and support, where people read a great deal and, in part, shaped their lives according to what they had read. As in the rest of Western Europe, the role of the printed word and the importance of the vernacular for purposes of communication, self-expression, and political and religious propaganda had been increasing since the sixteenth-century expansion in output of the printed word and the social-hierarchical struggle of the Reformation.

To be sure, the rise of vernacular literature in the North can only be dated from the beginning of the eighteenth century.

Its vigorous antecedents include both the written clerical literature in Latin and the orally transmitted Danish folk ballads, as well as many publications in Danish (and to a certain extent in German) of an ecclesiastical, political, and personal nature. When Ludvig Holberg (1684–1754),[1] who also wrote extensively in Latin, produced his Danish comedies in the early decades of the eighteenth century, there was a responsive public ready for them. More and more was written for popular consumption during the eighteenth century, and by the turn of the new century, Denmark could boast several writers of stature, notably Johannes Ewald (1743–81) and the young Adam Oehlenschläger (1779–1850) who, with others, gave to the Danish language a new air of poetic authority.

The rise of a Danish vernacular literature connoted a concomitant growth of nationalism (to become dominant in the nineteenth century) and a concern with domestic problems and local traditions. Oehlenschläger drew on Scandinavian antiquity for some of his most effective poetic and dramatic work. So, too, did the multi-faceted genius N. F. S. Grundtvig, who not only conceived the principle of the folk-high-school mentioned above but also was Denmark's most prolific writer of hymns. A champion of Danish and more generally Scandinavian culture, he time and again struck a blow for a Germanic renascence as well as pan-Scandinavian cultural unity. As the decades of the nineteenth century passed, more and more Danes took up their pens to write both imaginative and philosophical prose until, at the end of the century, Copenhagen became a vibrant and active literary center and Scandinavian literature spilled out over Western Europe and even much farther, to general acclaim. Hans Christian Andersen, Søren Kierkegaard, Henrik Ibsen, August Strindberg: these are names associated with world and not merely Scandinavian literature.

Critics have occasionally pointed out striking analogies between Pontoppidan and both the most popular Danish writer of the early nineteenth century, the short story writer and poet of the Jutland heath Steen Steensen Blicher (1782–1848) on the one hand and Denmark's most famous son, Hans Christian Andersen (1805–75) on the other. That Pontoppidan was familiar with works of both Blicher and Andersen is a foregone conclusion.

Even had he no literary bent, he would have been exposed to both writers during his school years. Since both Blicher and Andersen may be said to hold down a corner in the consciousness of every Dane, it probably is possible to identify in any Danish writer borrowed phrases and images used in describing domestic life, national customs, and the Danish landscape. It could scarcely be otherwise. This does not mean that, in the case of Pontoppidan, he was imitating either writer consciously. He was rather drawing on that fund of intellectual experience that his broad reading in Danish national literature had established. Andersen, Blicher, and somewhat later, Meïr Goldschmidt (1819–87) were no mean or insignificant models and sources of inspiration. Insofar as Pontoppidan reflects these, his older countrymen, he reflects classical Danish prose of the nineteenth century and imaginative writing which has maintained a lasting appeal to the general public, withstanding the erosion of aesthetic criticism for well over a century.

In short, Denmark possessed a rich literary endowment upon which the ambitious, inspired writer could draw. There were many writers from whom one could learn, and who could be a source of stimulation. Possibilities for success in being heard and being read were, to be sure, dependent on many other factors besides the existence of a plethora of writers. There had to be a relatively high standard of education, a well-developed book trade, an easy access to books through public libraries, and a possibility for an author to live from his pen, at least to the extent of having the necessary time and quiet to formulate his thoughts. Moreover, the social system had to accept the desirability of intellectual activity. All these conditions obtained in Denmark. Although Denmark was no utopia, it did offer many advantages to the imaginative writer at the end of the nineteenth century and enabled Henrik Pontoppidan and not a few of his contemporaries to pursue their muse. If imaginative writing did not suffice to make ends meet, there were many opportunities in journalistic endeavor. In addition, the successful and prestigious Danish writer could expect some support from the public purse in the form of annual stipends or poets' salaries, as they are now called.

With a mixture of boldness and caution, the young Henrik

Wellsprings

Pontoppidan used more than one medium for literary expression. He published short stories in periodicals, wrote sketches for journals and newspapers, and wrote short stories and short novels for separate publication. In his first few books, Pontoppidan gives a picture of country life in Denmark, notably the island of Zealand, Copenhagen's hinterland. He calls attention to particular facets of that life, including several widespread injustices. He has an eye for the picturesque as well as for the ironic in both rural landscape and rural society. One can safely use the term "naturalistic" about his books, for he was, like so many other writers of the 1880s, attempting to reproduce everyday reality as best he could—a contrast to the idealism and the fantasy that pervaded earlier Western European literature. The concept of naturalism in literature was, of course, widespread in the Western world at the end of the nineteenth century, and if we identify Pontoppidan as a naturalist we thereby classify him with a large group of writers whose source of inspiration was to a demonstrable extent the works of Emile Zola and the brothers Goncourt in France.

Pontoppidan had immediate predecessors on the Danish literary scene, however, who had already endeavored to do much the same that he undertook in the books he published between 1881 and 1890, but he surpassed them. The name of Sophus Schandorph may be mentioned in particular in this connection, for he must be considered Pontoppidan's immediate forerunner in choice of subject matter and in general attitude. Save to the literary historian, Schandorph is scarcely known today; but he is one of several Danish writers of the second half of the nineteenth century who produced a body of literature that provided Pontoppidan with literary models. The imaginative writer of greatest stature in the generation before Pontoppidan was Meïr Goldschmidt, an author whom Pontoppidan admired (as he relates in his autobiography).[2] For all his narrative talent, Goldschmidt was identified as a special kind of writer, viz. the speaker for Denmark's Jewish community. His best known work, *En Jøde* (*A Jew*, 1845), is a milestone in the development of literature in Denmark and a milestone in the history of Jewish literature in Europe as well, but only the clarity of style, not the subject matter, was reflected in Pontoppidan's works. Goldschmidt did not confine himself to Jewish material, however; his sketches of Danish country life are also noteworthy, and are similar to some of Pontoppidan's early sketches. In any case, Goldschmidt was one of the writers whom Pontoppidan had read when he himself started his literary career. Goldschmidt must be assumed to have contributed to Pontoppidan's ideal image of narrative and imaginative prose.

While various writers helped to mold Pontoppidan's style and to develop his poetic vision, they scarcely contributed to his selection of subjects. As noted, Pontoppidan is very much one with the naturalism of the late nineteenth century. Blicher, Goldschmidt, and Andersen had endeavored to evoke emotional responses in their readers, and had indeed done so, but by somewhat other means than writers of the 1870s and later, who were more concerned with representing reality than generating an emotional antiphony in their readers. The new spirit of the times demanded that attention be called to conditions that obtained at the moment and to the social, political, and economic problems of the day. This spirit, which had been developing since mid-century, was most pointedly formulated by the brilliant Danish critic Georg Brandes, who played the role of a harbinger of a new literature after his return from a sojourn abroad, particularly France, in 1871. It is from Brandes's famous lectures on the "literary currents" of the nineteenth century that the "breakthrough" of Scandinavian literature, that is, the expanding association of Scandinavian, particularly Danish, literature with the dominant, socially conscious new literature of France and England, is dated. While the view that Brandes single-handedly introduced a literary revolution into Scandinavia is but a convenient hyperbole, there is no disputing that he became the articulate spokesman of a new literature, and that many young writers rallied to a standard which also was a symbol for the victory of Darwinism and the weakening of the position of the established Christian religion in European society.

It is a curious fact that the writer who benefitted most from the Brandesian uproar, Jens Peter Jacobsen (1847–85)–a natural scientist who had translated Darwin into Danish–wrote two of the most significant modern, naturalistic novels, neither of which actually addressed itself to the "problems of the time." (They are, rather, penetrating psychological studies.) The writer who most nearly achieved Brandes's ideal was, however, not among the immediate followers of Brandes, did not hear the famous lectures, and did not subscribe to any explicit theory or pronouncement as to the nature of imaginative literature: Henrik Pontoppidan. Brandes and Pontoppidan nevertheless soon found that they were related in spirit, and they harbored a mutual respect and corresponded with one another for decades. In his prolific writings, Brandes typifies and synthesizes the currents of the new age. In lectures at the University of Copenhagen in 1871 and in later lectures and publications, he provided intellectual, social, and aesthetic stimulus for an entire generation.[3]

Among the foreign currents which Brandes mediated in Denmark, the most readily apparent is that of French aestheticism represented by St. Beuve and Hippolyte Taine. Brandes had written his doctoral dissertation on the subject of French aesthetics, and he was to apply the methods of St. Beuve in particular to his own criticism. Philosophically and religiously, he reflected the radical ideas of the German thinkers Ludwig Feuerbach and David Friedrich Strauss who had shaken the foundations of European Christianity before the middle of the nineteenth century and who contributed to the acceptance of nonbelief and agnosticism. Brandes was also aware of the political radicalism identified as socialism (now, but not then, inextricably bound up with the name of Marx); but more important to him was the current of English thought that was identified above all with the utilitarianism of John Stuart Mill. Brandes himself translated Mill's book on utilitarianism in 1872.

The pervasiveness of Brandes's criticism and the central position which he enjoyed in his own time is suggested by the role which he was to play at the turn of the century under the name of "Dr. Nathan" in Henrik Pontoppidan's best known novel, *Lykke-Per*. Some of Pontoppidan's courage as a socially conscious writer doubtless derived from Brandes's inspiration. Pontoppidan nevertheless remained very much a Danish writer in the sense that his subject matter was domestic and that his affinity for Danish life, however he might at times castigate his countrymen, and for the Danish landscape was unmistakable. The foreign writers who enjoyed such prestige in Brandes's pantheon are not visible in the world of Pontoppidan's creative imagination. Henrik Ibsen and Bjørnstjerne Bjørnson are the only apparent exceptions to this observation, though both Norwegians were actually part and parcel of the contemporary literary scene in Denmark.

CHAPTER 2

Impressions into Words

I The End is a Beginning

IN his memoirs, Henrik Pontoppidan tells of his debut as an author. It might be called a split level debut: he sent a collection of short stories in manuscript to the critic Otto Borchsenius, who was editor of the popular journal *Ude og Hjemme* (best rendered as *At Home and Abroad*). Borchsenius selected the story "Et Endeligt" ("A Death," or more precisely, "The End of a Life") for publication in September of 1881. The story was well received, and Borchsenius, who was a figure of importance on the contemporary literary scene, encouraged Pontoppidan. Because of his recommendation, Pontoppidan very soon thereafter received an offer from a lesser-known Copenhagen publisher (Andreas Schou) to issue the entire collection of stories in book form. This was the volume *Stækkede Vinger* (*Clipped Wings*), which appeared late the same year, 1881. The publication of this first volume by Pontoppidan marked the major turning point in his life, for with the modest royalty he received, he married and apparently made the irrevocable decision to live from his pen.

Like many of his early tales, "Et Endeligt" is an indictment of human cruelty in everyday life, of the disregard of the rights of the underprivileged, and, more specifically, of the failure to recognize the need of old people for love and understanding. An old man named Niels Ingvor and his halting mare are merely a source of mirth for the well-to-do. The impoverished old man, his wife, and their piteous granddaughter Johanna accept the meanness of their existence as their immutable and unhappy lot. Because of their inevitable fate they do not expect sympathy from others nor understanding of their tears. The two old people must accept the indignities of old age without so much as a token of appreciation from the society to which they contributed to their best abilities. The old mare had labored with its master for twenty-seven long years to provide the count—who owned the land the old man worked— the clergyman, and the deacon "their due."

As her grandfather lies dying, Johanna tries in vain to get the local physician to attend him. After an unpardonable delay, the physician finally goes out to her wagon, the same old wagon and tired mare, only to refuse to be driven in such an "antique" vehicle. He shows no more compassion for the helpless trio than do the count, the clergyman, and the deacon. After the old man's death, his widow is doomed to the poorhouse, and the granddaughter is sent out to earn her way in the "vast, bewildering world." On the way to the poorhouse, grandmother and granddaughter are not spared the heartbreak of viewing part of the auction of their few worldly goods including the beloved mare, bought for a few shillings by a local butcher in order to translate the old nag into "fresh young beef."

Since "Et Endeligt" was Pontoppidan's first published work, it warrants special scrutiny, but today that is not as easy a task as it might seem. The versions of the story that are now available differ greatly from the story that Pontoppidan offered to the reading public in 1881. This fact provides the first, striking example of Pontoppidan's marked and lasting penchant for reworking everything he wrote and published. While many authors have revised early works, few have been as consistent, insistent, and thorough as was Pontoppidan, with whom rewriting might almost be considered an obsession. Sixty years after making his debut, Pontoppidan was still engaged in rewriting and shortening—this time his own autobiography. After having published four volumes of memoirs between 1933 and 1940, he was to rewrite them in one short volume issued in the year of his death, 1943. He retold the story of his early life in such different ways that a reader must choose his biographical reality; the data of the first version do not always correspond to those of the final version.

In point of fact, the versions of "Et Endeligt" are so different that it is difficult to compare them, for the changes are not

Impressions into Words

merely those of style, diction, and syntax. Although the nucleus of the story remains the same, sentences of the original have been omitted and other sentences of quite a different nature inserted. In the final version of the tale, published separately in 1904 (and later incorporated into various collections of Pontoppidan's short stories), there is no doubt that the author has attempted to improve his style by more careful diction, more cautious use of hyperbole, and more precise description and dialogue. He has also revised the lengths of the paragraphs.

The original version begins by using somewhat exceptional word order and repetition: "Out of the large, large spruce woods rolled an old, old vehicle — as if out of another century. The wagon was a little, low wooden cart, the age of which it would be fruitless to try to guess. But the man had to be between ninety and three hundred; — and that the poor, bony thing which shuffled along in front with small, stiff hops, once had been a shiny brown mare, one might soon guess after searching around a bit in natural history."

Compare now the final version, from the year 1904:

"There rumbled an old vehicle out of a large, dark spruce woods. The wagon was a little, low wooden box, which seemed to date from heathen times; the man who sat on the wagon seat with the reins hanging loose in his hand was visibly not born yesterday; and that the poor bony creature, which shuffled along in front with small, stiff hops, ever had been a real horse, one had difficulty imagining."

The language of the later version strikes us at once as more literary, as well as syntactically more traditional. The image of the driver has been expanded. Not only the two brief paragraphs cited above have been condensed but the first three have been amalgamated into one paragraph. At least one change in diction shows a greater sensitivity toward the sound of words on Pontoppidan's part. In the first version the word "hop" is used to describe the motion of the horse, but the horse is at once identified as a mare—in Danish *Hoppe*. To avoid the repetition of *hop* in *Hoppe*, Pontoppidan substituted the word *Hest* ("horse"). Instead of an unwanted internal rhyme, only the alliterative *h* remains.

Although brief sections of the story remain unchanged, alterations such as shown above are representative of Pontoppidan's reworking of his own narrative style after the passage of a quarter of a century. During that time he had written many books, large and small, and had become established as one of Denmark's leading authors. Yet it is to be remembered that he had not achieved a style which satisfied him; what he wrote for the first time in 1904 would also be revised, although not as drastically as his first story.

The title of *Stækkede Vinger* (*Clipped Wings*) suggests the attitude that was to inform not only the stories in that volume but a series of narratives in both novella and novel form that Pontoppidan was to produce during the next ten years. The individuals to whom he is calling the reader's attention have suffered for reasons propounded by the theorists of naturalist literature in the nineteenth century: they have been adversely affected by both their heredity and their milieu. The immediate source of inspiration for his work is not apparent, although the book was not so strikingly original that it seemed an exceptional publication in the 1880s. In addition to "Et Endeligt" the volume includes two "sketches" (as Pontoppidan identifies them): "Efter Ballet" ("After the Ball") and "Tête à tête," as well as a lengthy story which occupies 170 of the book's 250 pages: "Kirkeskuden" ("The Ship Model" or more precisely, "The Votive Ship"). This last story was actually written first, a fact that may explain its loose construction and multiplicity of plot.

The two sketches take place in the Danish capital and, unlike most of Pontoppidan's other tales, which are set in rural Zealand, can be identified with the drawing room. Settings and action are not distinctive for Pontoppidan; the social anguish depicted through the fates of two major figures, one a young man, the other a young woman, for whom in each case marriage is the way of practical salvation, is not an uncommon theme. Models or analogues could be found in the work of various writers, foreign as well as Danish. Nevertheless, Pontoppidan did demonstrate that he could write this type of narrative successfully, but did not think highly enough of the two tales ever to have them reprinted. "Kirkeskuden" was another matter. Sixteen years later the story was separately published in revised form. In the original version, Pontoppidan essentially

Impressions into Words

tells three stories, all relating to social need. The first is of Ane, a clumsy girl who is taken advantage of by an inconsiderate man whom she kills when he will not marry her. As a result, she is committed to ten-year's imprisonment. The second is of her child, a pitiful youngster whom the community wants to support only at the minimal expense, and who is foisted upon the local clergyman and his wife, who have no children. The third is of Ane's rejected first suitor, who lives in squalor until he is drawn into a profitable scheme of thievery after Ane is released from prison. The central figure of the story is Ane's son Ove. To his foster mother he is a godsend and she showers her affection upon him, but his foster father, the impractical and psychologically myopic clergyman, has no comprehension of Ove's real needs. He is quite ready to imagine the worst about Ove when suspicion for the thefts (for which in fact Ane is responsible) falls upon him. The suspicion results from Ove's fascination with a ship model hanging in the church. He wants to try it out in water, and has no evil intent. After secluding himself in church after services, he removes the ship. By chance, at almost the same time, his mother, unbeknownst to him, steals the church's poorbox. After losing the ship on a small ocean bay, Ove is afraid to go home and is subsequently assumed to be guilty of a crime which he did not commit. He is shipped off to be a member of the crew on a schooner belonging to his mother's partner-in-crime. An unexpected fortunate turn of events in the last seven lines of the story (Ove, declared drowned, returns for the burial of his foster father) robs the narrative of the impact it might otherwise have had. The attitude of the boy in the story presents a parallel to that of the young Pontoppidan as we learn of it both as a reflex in the first volume of his novel *Lykke-Per* and later in his memoirs.

Pontoppidan's first book had been sufficiently well received that he was encouraged to continue as a writer. In his second book, the novel *Sandinge Menighed* (*Sandinge Parish*, 1883) he gives a broad but ironic picture of village life in Denmark. For the first time Pontoppidan deals with the transition from village life to life in the capital. This theme will be of great importance in the first volume of his *magnum opus*, the autobiographically colored *Lykke-Per*. The clergyman in "The Ship Model" suggests the figure of Pastor Emanuel Hansted, the central character in Pontoppidan's first multi-volume novel, *Det forjættede Land* (*The Promised Land*, 1891-95).

II A Lay Sermon

Sandinge Menighed (*Sandinge Parish*, 1883), Pontoppidan's second book and first novel, is a mixture of numerous elements also found in several of his later works: social satire, irony, caricature of human weaknesses, the discord between the ideal and the real, the significance of landscape as a symbolic element in narrative, and the position of Grundtvigianism in Danish society. In *Sandinge Menighed* these elements are not very well assimilated; it is as if the author wanted to put too much into a relatively short novel, a characteristic of the inexperienced writer. Despite such apparent weakness, the story is nevertheless compelling by virtue of the forcefulness of its language, the realistic quality of its descriptions, and its ironic humor. As was to be the case later in Pontoppidan's multi-volume novel *Lykke Per*, some insight is given into several levels of society.

The story begins in a Danish village where an intolerable familial situation exists. Boel, the mistreated, illegitimate daughter of a hypocritical schoolteacher, is sent to Copenhagen. There she benefits from the generosity of Mrs. Gylling, who enjoys visions of grandeur by holding a tiresome salon in which she goes out of her way to be condescending to visiting provincials and other unsophisticated persons in the Danish capital. Her insufferable son has had himself elected the chairman of a committee intending to champion the cause of the Danish peasant by composing an address from the Danish students to the Danish peasant. Much is made of the Danish students nominally reaching out their hands to the Danish peasant in a spirit of comradeship. The mood of Mrs. Gylling's salon is set by a large picture of N. F. S. Grundtvig on the wall—the visionary, partisan, and demagogic Grundtvig who conceived the folk-high-school and who worked in various ways for the general elevation of popular knowledge during much of the nineteenth century. The fraudulence of Mrs. Gylling's benevolent pose becomes apparent when her son believes that he has fallen in love with the mistreated village girl living with his mother. The mere thought of such a union the mother dismisses as impossible and unthinkable, since it would destroy her own ambitions for her son.

Pontoppidan's satire and sarcasm are directed not only at social hypocrisy but also at a type of writing which he considered affected, such as that of the great Danish naturalist and stylist, Jens Peter Jacobsen. One of the verbal snapshots that Pontoppidan has inserted into the main current of the narrative is a lengthy passage ascribed to a contemporary writer in which the use of adjectives of color is carried to an extreme. A unique sensitivity toward color is one of the most easily identifiable traits of Jacobsen's prose. One observes that Pontoppidan and Jacobsen actually represent two different attitudes toward naturalism in literature. Pontoppidan felt that verisimilitude is best achieved in dialogue and in the depiction of everyday situations, whereas Jacobsen stressed detailed description enhanced by a large and precise vocabulary. Nonetheless, at the same time he was an incisive psychologist, a fact with which Pontoppidan could have had no quarrel.

Recurrent reference to the portrait of Grundtvig on the wall at Mrs. Gylling's suggests Pontoppidan's own ambivalent position vis-à-vis the Grundtvigian cause. As noted, he had already instructed at the folk-high-school of which one of his brothers was principal. Grundtvigianism is not the only autobiographical overtone in *Sandinge Menighed*. Pontoppidan had also been moved to attempt a fusion of urban and rural culture. In this spirit he had married his first wife who was, in more than one sense of the word, a country girl. There was no doubt about Pontoppidan's sincerity in his early years, but he seems early to have gained considerable insight into the potential difficulty which could be engendered by an attempt to dismiss class differences and to disregard the contrast between urban and rural culture and the social implications of such differences and contrast.

The leaders of the student movement in the novel are motivated only by a desire for personal aggrandizement and not by any conviction of the need for a more democratic society.

The schoolteacher embodies not only human failings in a man who should represent an ideal figure for his charges but also the prevalence of religious cant. He retreats into pious phrases and the appeal of hymns out of sheer laziness.

The novel is not simply a depiction of country life, for its settings are urban as well as rural. It is a lay sermon to Pontoppidan's contemporaries, a criticism of weaknesses in society by means of imaginative writing, selected dramatic scenes, incisive imagery, and explicit depiction. It concentrates into a relatively few *personæ dramatis* conditions in need of recognition and amelioration.

The young Pontoppidan was perspicacious. Whereas many of his contemporaries believed in what could not be—chiefly because of their fond hopes and will to believe that everything would after all turn out for the best—he was not deceived. He wanted to hold up a mirror to his fellow citizens, but in such a way that a multitude of faults was exposed. Such is the zeal of the young and not always effective reformer, an observation that Pontoppidan himself suggests to the reader at the end of his narrative, for the basic problems remain. The cyclical quality of life and the recurrent nature of social difficulties are symbolized by Boel's return to the village of Sandinge and her abused and abusing mother. She has gained understanding of the difficulties that the mother had to face earlier, but now the mother's burdens have been increased immeasurably after her husband has been invalided because of an accident at work.

One notes that the novel is concentrated upon Sandinge not only as a community but also as a parish. The ecclesiastical overtone is unmistakable, the irony inherent. A parish should mean a community sharing a common belief and a common concern for its members. The parish in Sandinge, however, is at best a clerical technicality. The ineffective clergyman of the parish is neither a leader nor a guide, neither an effective pastor nor a pillar of strength. He may be filled with pity for the downtrodden among his communicants, but this does them little practical good.

Pontoppidan was not writing at a comfortable distance from the scenes that he elected to depict. While there is an element of caricature in the persons and situations that he developed, he was writing on the basis of observation and experience. He knew the society in a rural village on the island of Zealand firsthand, after he had lived as a student in Copenhagen for several years. He had chosen a rural existence over an urban one, doubtless for a variety of reasons. He wanted to be closer to natural surroundings; he wanted to escape the artificiality of life in a large city; he wanted to feel himself more the master of his own fate and to be more himself than the strictures of living in a metropolis would permit.

If Pontoppidan moved into the country because he assumed that life there would be more nearly guileless or even idyllic, he was soon disabused of any such misconception. His villagers can be as greedy and deceptive as any urban worldling, and there is quite as much abuse of human rights in the one place as the other. There can be an abyss between the words and actions of a petty rural autocrat as well as those of an urban social climber. There are nevertheless good people, naive people—and exploited people—both places. The novel begins with the girl Boel's being inhumanly treated by her mother—but Boel's ill treatment goads nobody in the community to action, least of all her real father. A schoolteacher, he takes refuge behind his religious conversion and false piety to create an artificial distance between the thoughtless, sensuous young man he once was and the sly and self-serving creature he has become.

In hiding behind his pseudo-religiosity, the schoolteacher is a forerunner of the many figures associated with organized religion in the works of Pontoppidan. They call into question the sincerity of the reader's own convictions and the usefulness of the established church. They are living monuments to ecclesiastical vested interests and the willingness to abide by the status quo, whatever abuses may be apparent. If the schoolteacher suggests the lack of character in more traditional organized religion, he also implies, although not as clearly as Mrs. Gylling, the wordiness of the nineteenth-century movement of national enlightenment known as Grundtvigianism. As we already have mentioned, Pontoppidan had for a time functioned within the Grundtvigian movement, as a teacher at his brother

Morten's folk-high-school—and the folk-high-schools were always the stronghold of Grundtvigianism. He had necessarily also observed the late nineteenth-century efforts at pan-Scandinavianism which were closely related to the Grundtvigian movement and the essentially conservative efforts to create a bond of understanding between the Danish peasant—who, because of more favorable social conditions, no longer could be considered a peasant in the same sense as those peasants of various European countries to the south—and the Danish intellectual. Pontoppidan did not scoff at the idealism which engendered the idea of a spiritual unity between farmers and students, but he saw how such an idea can become warped and misused when an attempt is made to put it into practice, how the naive are misled by the conniving, how personal ambitions spoil simple enthusiasms and good intentions.

Otto Borchsenius, Pontoppidan's early critical benefactor, wrote about *Sandinge Menighed* upon its appearance in 1883: "There lies in the plan of this narrative doubtless the raw material for an entire social novel of no little interest...."[1] This assessment is easy to agree with in retrospect. Borchsenius's positive critique was nevertheless tempered by the observation that Pontoppidan "had not yet learned to construct a unified work of art" for too much of the narrative was episodic, "not to say in bits and pieces."

CHAPTER 3

Iconoclastic Pastoral

THE same year that *Sandinge Menighed* was published, Pontoppidan issued a collection of short stories called *Landsbybilleder (Village Sketches)*. Whereas *Sandinge Menighed* had been published by a lesser-known firm, *Landsbybilleder* was accepted for publication by the Gyldendal Publishing Company, which was and is Denmark's oldest and most prestigious publisher, and at that time the most influential publisher in Scandinavia. In his memoirs, Pontoppidan tells of his own surprise at meeting the director of Gyldendal, Frederik V. Hegel, on the street, and being treated with admiration and respect because of the impression that his first book had made upon Hegel. Acceptance by Gyldendal was almost the equivalent of continued success in literary circles in Denmark. In retrospect, it is not difficult to see the embryo of much of Pontoppidan's later work in this collection of short stories. Here as elsewhere, there is considerable emphasis on description, not purely for its own sake, but for the ironic overtones that can be worked into description in a tongue-in-cheek, matter-of-fact kind of way.

The stories constitute an exposé of village life, a refutation of the concept of rural idyll. Thus the irony in the title of "Rural Idyll" (which Pontoppidan was to rewrite simply as "Idyll" in 1899). The wealthy farmer's son, whose father's generosity is supposedly shown by the amount of food and drink he supplies his subjugated coparishioners at the annual harvest festival, takes advantage of a young hired man's fiancée. There is really nothing the girl or her fiancé can do about it, since they can only look forward to being economically dependent on their exploiters. "Arv" ("Inheritance") is a preliminary version of the short novel *Lille Rødhætte (Little Red*

Riding-Hood) written in 1900. Pontoppidan was to reissue it, with the central character's name as the title, *Thora van Deken*, in 1922. In essence the story—of perjury, albeit understandable, committed for the sake of an inheritance—is the same as that contained in the later short novel, although Pontoppidan's earlier resolution is the more melodramatic: the woman who has perjured herself loses her mind as a result. The intrinsically dramatic quality of the story is attested by its having been reworked for the stage by Pontoppidan and Hjalmar Bergstrøm (1868–1914) in 1913 and its subsequently having been made into a Swedish film.[1]

"En Kærlighedshistorie" ("A Love Story") is a specimen of a continuing argument in Pontoppidan's writing: the contrast between a sensibly arranged marriage and romantic love, where passion is viewed as the ultimate criterion. The pair that more or less (chiefly for economic reasons) is forced into a marriage which superficially seems to be ill-matched, achieves a happy coexistence, whereas the clergyman's daughter, who enjoys social and economic advantages, marries the man of her choice—only to end up in disenchantment. This particular story must have been something of a surprise to its readers. Free choice in matters of erotic love was part of the times. There was something unusual about a twenty-six-year-old author apparently speaking up for a conservative tradition in love and marriage when the mood of the day encouraged the so-called rights of passion.

"Vinterbillede" ("Winter Portrait") is both humorous and biting in its portrayal of men of the cloth. First, the piteous Pastor Faltring, whose function as a clergyman is meaningless in a congregation that comes to church in a show of local camaraderie only when the bishop makes his annual visitation. Second, the bishop himself, whose myopic interpretation of the Christian faith causes him to cashier Faltring because of the latter's unwillingness to persecute a few followers of a premillenarian sect whose modest dwelling the churchmen pass on a postprandial walk. Even Faltring's annual sermon for the bishop (always the same, the only sermon from his years in training that received a commendation) declines in quality in the bishop's mind. Here is an early example of Pontoppidan's digs at narrow-minded Lutheranism, at "the church and its men" (the subject of a vigorously worded pamphlet Pontoppidan wrote thirty-one years later).

Pontoppidan was never to rework or republish the final story of the collection, "En Fiskerrede" ("A Fisherman's Nest"). It is an acid commentary on human greed, put into the past, perhaps to alleviate criticism of its extremism, but also to suggest that conditions today are not identical with those of an earlier age. Fishermen exploit unabashedly and inhumanely the misfortune of a ship and its crew in need. The "nest" of the title suggests a nest of vultures rather than any cozy nest of strapping fishermen.

Two years after the publication of *Landsbybilleder*, Pontoppidan rewrote "En Kærlighedshistorie" as a short novel and titled it *Ung Elskov* (*Young Love*, 1885). In the short novel we meet the same situation and the same persons from the story: Grethe, forced into marriage by her mother—in contrast to her childhood playmate, the clergyman's daughter Rebekka, who was allowed to follow the dictates of passion—finds happiness in a marriage not originally based on love.

In the first version of *Ung Elskov*, Pontoppidan composed a variation on the theme of practical marriage versus romantic love, again with disastrous consequences for the girl who dreams of love's pleasures instead of accepting a stable place in society when marriage is proposed by an honest suitor. The first version is the more straightforward tale, and suggests the tenets of the naturalistic school regarding heredity and milieu. In the second and more readily accessible version, from the year 1906, the story is compounded by the introduction of a narrator who once had an attachment to the girl's mother when she was young. The mother had unexpectedly been seduced by a travelling peddler; pregnancy and the birth of a red-haired daughter, later seduced herself by a travelling student, resulted. With charity and sorrow, the narrator follows the daughter's development until the juncture where she kills her own fiancé when he tries to take advantage of her in the woods one night. Whereas the mother lives to bear her shame, the daughter succumbs to her fears and her conscience, becomes mentally deranged, and ends a suicide in the mill pond.

The 1906 version of the story makes Pontoppidan's intent clearer, quite aside from the restructuring of the narrative resulting from the introduction of an interested narrator. Both versions make extended use of descriptions of nature, the details of the second version demonstrating that such descriptions are neither casual nor incidental to Pontoppidan. They provide the background and mood, serving a symbolic function as well as making visible the milieu in which the action takes place. The description of Jutland and the characters who people its bleak landscape is reminiscent of Denmark's great early regionalist writer Steen Steensen Blicher, poet of the heath and the most popular Danish narrator in the early nineteenth century. In the second version of *Ung Elskov*, Pontopiddan seems to be making a conscious effort to write like Blicher, without directly imitating him.

This is, to be sure, only one characteristic of Pontoppidan's narrative art at an early stage, but it is not insignificant. It identifies his position in the development of Danish literature during the nineteenth and early twentieth centuries and suggests both a continuity and a certain national, domestic quality of that literature. The national orientation of the narrative is emphasized in this book by an intercalation of modern folk tales which have no direct bearing on the development of the central story.

Secondarily, Pontoppidan touches upon the inadequacies of society and the prevalence of social injustice, particularly in the 1906 version. The later version is pervaded by a skepticism about the sort of love-making that belongs more in novels than in the real, practical world. The story is a conglomerate rather than a compound: the several love stories do not fit together very well, though one might interpret this as an attempt to avoid the artificiality of standard imaginative literature, where there are no loose ends and every situation or set of characters neatly dovetails with the next.

CHAPTER 4

Essays in Morality

THE common denominator of the early stories and short novels is the position of the individual in need of tolerant understanding who is subjected to, and subjugated by, an intolerant society. The multiple concerns of the 1880s are also echoed and articulated in Pontoppidan's works.

Pontoppidan's short novel *Mimoser* (*Mimosas,* 1886) was apparently written as a contribution to the great discussion on sexual morals that took place in Scandinavia in the 1880s.[1] To be sure, the story can be read from two points of view. The two young ladies who are the central characters of the tale are indeed mimosas, that is, sensitive plants, so sensitive that when the husband of each is discovered to have had a passing affair with another woman, each sister impulsively terminates her marriage. While at the beginning of the story the sisters are sympathetically depicted, their reactions vis-à-vis their respective husbands seem foolishly abrupt. Each woman succeeds only in destroying her own future. We can understand the dismay and sense of bitter disappointment when a woman discovers that her husband had not led a chaste life, but we should consider the possibility that a husband may react with consternation and rue the effect of his infidelity upon his wife, as is the case in Pontoppidan's story. Pontoppidan makes clear where he stands only with an unanticipated concluding chapter that consists of a letter from one of the husbands. He writes from Rome to his mother in Copenhagen, reporting that he is living with his mistress and enjoying life. Despite a feeling of guilt after having strayed from the path of virtue and despite his efforts to regain his wife's affection, he has gone back to his mistress because his wife will no longer have him.

The plot is straightforward, though the reaction of the two women is extreme. As clear a position as Pontoppidan seems to us to have taken here, that clarity was not apparent to all of his contemporaries. Some sensed an acceptance of the position taken by the Norwegian poet and agitator Bjørnstjerne Bjørnson (1832–1910) who in theory, although scarcely in practice, was a champion of monogamy and chastity.

While the title figure in Pontoppidan's next short novel, *Isbjørnen* (*The Polar Bear*, 1887), a clergyman, is not involved with any marital problems, he is a striking example of the clash between the eccentric individual and a society which demands conformity because of lack of insight and courage. The "polar bear" is a forerunner of the "little man" in the story "Gallows Hill at Ilum" contained in the collection *Skyer* (*Clouds*) in 1890. Both are hopelessly grotesque, although both keep to their principles. The clergyman, who has spent most of his adult life in Greenland, had been given his charge because he was a hopeless student of theology at the University of Copenhagen and, purely for the sake of a stipend, had agreed to serve in Greenland after completing his course at the university. In Greenland, he identified himself with the Eskimo community that he served and grew to appreciate the Eskimo way of life. After his return to Denmark he cut a peculiar figure with his carelessness of dress and manners, some of which derived from habits he acquired in Greenland. He shocks the ecclesiastical establishment, not only because of his appearance but also because of the popularity he eventually enjoys among his parishioners and even beyond his parish. He becomes a potential threat to his brothers of the cloth, who translate their own envy into charges based on his unwillingness to be like them. Ultimately they create a situation in which there is to be a visitation by a bishop leading to some sort of reprimand for the Greenland clergyman. Like the little man in "Gallows Hill," after he has failed to widen the horizons of the inhabitants of Ilum, the "polar bear" elects to depart. Where the little man speaks at length with the nominal narrator of the story and expounds his philosophy, the "polar bear" expresses his position very simply by writing in chalk on the door of his house, "You have the tyrants you deserve."

Essays in Morality

Fra Hytterne (*From the Huts*, 1887), is a second collection of "Village Sketches"; indeed, it carries the subtitle "New Village Sketches." Pontoppidan had become increasingly aware of the social and political malaise that existed in Denmark at the time. The five stories in the new collection may be characterized as intentional contributions to the literature of social consciousness. Pontoppidan is concerned with the injustice of poverty thrust upon the innocent and he writes with touching understanding of the characters in his book. This may be exemplified by the story 'Naadsensbrød" ("Charity") about an old woman who was forced to leave her ramshackle home in an endeavor to improve her lot. The reader is made to feel that an injustice has been done and to understand that the only humane action would have been to leave the old woman in her miserable surroundings where she was at peace with the world.

The other stories in the collection exemplify difference between the rights and privileges money obtains and the bitter dregs of poverty. Thus a girl who has become pregnant is not permitted to marry her lover because his mother has other, vain ambitions for him. When she returns from Copenhagen, pregnant once more, but this time in possession of a fat bank account, there is no lack of suitors, including the father of her first child. The reader is relieved to learn she spurns him in favor of a sensible union with a widower. This tale, "Hans and Trine," is a story of seduction, but with a happy end, an example of the exploitation of an innocent country girl with the wry twist that the seducer ultimately is meted out a kind of punishment while the girl becomes the happy mother of a growing family. The first part of the story reads almost as a classical example of the literature of social consciousness. Trine's mother Mariane is no model woman. She is a widow without means, the mother of many children, and a friend of the bottle. Coming from such a milieu, her children (we hear only of daughters) can be presumed to be compromised in advance on their life's way. Different daughters return home from time to time to bear children conceived out of wedlock, burdening the community with a generation of grandchildren, although Mariane has from time to time assisted some of the newborn to a quick trip to the other world "and afterwards blamed it on the good Lord."

Trine is an exception among Mariane's daughters, reticent toward the opposite sex because of an incident that took place when she was fifteen which she herself did not fully understand. Her reticence is finally overcome by the handsome, blond Hans, who becomes the father of her child. Because of his own will to believe his mother's evil tongue, he refuses to marry Trine, even though he has to admit paternity of her child and make an annual payment for the child's upkeep.

More poignant is the story "Knokkelmanden" ("The Bone Man") that contrasts the honest striving of simple folk and the seeming injustice of fate. Here is a social consciousness of a different kind than in the story "Naadsensbrød." Pontoppidan is not dealing with inhumanity and thoughtlessness, the sort of social consciousness that would be taken up later by Martin Andersen-Nexø (1869–1954) and other writers of a similar persuasion who believed that certain changes in the economic and social system could alleviate human woe. The early Pontoppidan may also have tended to this belief. He was certainly to expound metaphorically the evils of political repression in the collection of stories entitled *Skyer* (*Clouds*) in 1890. In "Knokkelmanden," however, good, hardworking people are beset by a force apparently beyond their ken and control: fatal sickness. Within the strictures of their own philosophy and the mores of their community, a man and his wife have hewn to the most admirable principles. They have been self-sacrificing; they have lived frugally and honestly; they have exploited every bit of soil that was theirs to work; they have been true to their Christian faith.

Nevertheless, it is quite possible that their very lack of enlightenment and their naiveté regarding hygiene and disease, or, to put it more bluntly, their ignorance combined with superstitious belief, is the real cause of Ane's death, although from the description of her symptoms it is apparent that she is dying from a cancer that is beyond help from the medical profession. Be that as it may, she seeks adequate medical advice only when her case clearly is hopeless and she has but a short time left to live. In the early stages of her illness she tried every remedy that well-meaning neighbors foisted upon her, but of course without any beneficial result. Pontoppidan draws no moral in his tale. The reader can react as he sees fit, either by shaking his head out of pity for a good woman who is struck down by what seems to be random fatal illness, or by observing that a more enlightened attitude toward illness and some comprehension for the need of immediate medical attention might have made a difference in Ane's life, and the life of her husband and their only child.

Typical for Pontoppidan are the descriptions which provide the setting for the story, both the interpretive natural images and the insight into the social patterns of the rural population. Also typical is the contrast between the rural and the urban dweller, the man of the soil and the highly educated, demonstrated in particular by striking differences in conversation; a paucity of words versus an ability to articulate easily (though without necessarily expressing substance).

The story "Et Grundskud" ("A Deathblow") is a bitterly humorous analogue of human misery and death, where sickness and death befall not a human being, but a hog. The hog is central to the life of the family that owns it, particularly to the family's economic well-being. The two annual high points in the life of Jacob Hansen and his family are the acquisition of a suckling pig at the Candlemas fair every February and the slaughter of the same animal, now a weighty hog, after Martinmas in November. The whole family looked forward with excitement to the acquisition of the four-week-old pig, of whose ability to grow and be fat "so to speak their entire existence depended." They followed its development with hope and pride, rejoicing at every added pound of weight.

This particular year's pig was full of promise. It grew and grew so that its fat sides hung down and made everyone's mouth water at the thought of that which might come. It was finally so swollen with fat and meat that it could scarcely move; it weighed 200 pounds. But a short time before it was to be slaughtered, it developed a serious rash and was obviously critically ill. Little time was wasted and the veterinarian was called. He prescribed medication that did no good. The end seemed near. With cold sweat on his brow, Jacob Hansen sat by his hog and wondered how fate could be so unkind. If such a blow must fall, then perhaps better one of the children; there were many children. For what should they do, if they lost the single hog? It meant their entire welfare; it was their only hope for the long winter. Jacob's wife sobbed; the children looked about with frightened eyes. All were aware of the seriousness of the moment, but to no avail. Fate was not kind.

Although many of Pontoppidan's stories have a viable ethical substance, other early novellas are merely entertaining and anecdotal. They depend on well-worn devices in order to generate suspense. An example of such a work, not blessed by Pontoppidan's redeeming virtues, is the story "Vildt" ("Wild Game"), one of the two short novels that constitute the volume *Natur* (*Nature*, 1890). A student from Copenhagen spends some time in a country inn, falls in with a gang of poachers, is briefly attracted to the wife of an absent fisherman, and takes part in the capture of an escaped convict.

The other novella in the volume, "En Bonde" ("A Farmer"), has many of the elements of the early *Landsbybilleder* in that it tells the story of an upright farmer whose too many children ultimately force him to sell the family farm and divide the price among them. Sentimentality rather than indignation predominates. It is no longer the social order at fault, but simply human character. Avarice is the source of evil. The unappreciative children have a different, more urban and worldly set of values than their earthbound, peasant father. Having sold the farm, he is pained by the way its new owner works the soil to increase its yield and by the way he treats, or mistreats, the horses.

Pontoppidan may be faulted for a tendency to the melodramatic in the early stories, but he was wilfully dramatizing the social injustices and deplorable ignorance he saw about him. Without voices being raised in protest, they could not be ameliorated. He was one of many writers in the late nineteenth and early twentieth centuries who were indignant about social conditions mutely crying out for change. They needed the articulation of a writer like Pontoppidan to rouse the public conscience and contribute to the spirit of change that in the course of a few decades was to lessen class difference, improve the lot of the simple worker and servant, and help engender a social consciousness for which the Scandinavian countries have become famous since World War I.

The short novel *Spøgelser* (*Ghosts*, 1888) is also critical of

Essays in Morality

the social order that in particular gave precious few rights to unmarried women who did not have the good fortune to be well-endowed with worldly goods. The title's echo of Ibsen's play is rather misleading, for the narrative is actually a love story with a happy ending. The daughter of a recently deceased clergyman is sent to a nearby estate—the owners of which had aroused her father's scorn—to be a companion to an old noblewoman. Although her life at first seems irreparably shattered, a new basis for existence is generated through the mutual attraction between her and the estate's gamekeeper, who turns out to be the young count of the estate's noble family and a man who properly rejects the artificial life of the manor house itself. Although there seems to be an indication that the young count is mentally unbalanced, love conquers all, and, with a *salto mortale* to which Friedrich Schiller would have objected, the loving pair ends up in Seville, Spain, "and the air is filled with the intoxicating odor of flowers and fruit." The reader who is accustomed to Pontoppidan's seriousness and frequent use of a tragic turn of events is somewhat disconcerted by an ending that suggests light romance rather than realistic narrative with credible ethical substance. One cannot help wondering whether *Spøgelser* is something of a potboiler. Despite the melodramatic nature of the story and the cloying conclusion, *Spøgelser* enjoyed a larger audience than many of Pontoppidan's other short novels. It has appeared in Swedish, Dutch, and German translations, but Pontoppidan never let it be reprinted in Danish.

CHAPTER 5

Political Parables

THE third collection of short stories which Pontoppidan published was *Skyer* (*Clouds*, 1890). It is his most significant and most widely read. The earlier collections of stories concern themselves with life in the country and depict social conditions and injustices from which various individuals suffer. *Skyer* comprises an oblique but vigorous attack upon the untenable political conditions under which Denmark suffered in the 1880s, as is indicated by the subtitle of the book: "Sketches from the days of the Provisional Government."

Starting in 1877 and for several years in the 1880s, Denmark had been governed not by parliamentary procedures, but by a series of provisional decrees issued by the authoritarian Prime Minister J. B. S. Estrup, who was in reality functioning as a dictator. The stories in *Skyer* indicate that Pontoppidan was as incensed by the unwillingness of his countrymen to organize and act against this outrage as he was by the mode of government itself.

The first story (also the prologue of the book), "Ilum Galgebakke" ("Gallows Hill at Ilum"), has become a classic in Danish literature because of its political satire, its historical value, and the masterful style which here is clearly identifiable as Pontoppidan's own. The central figure, the "little man," is grotesque to the point of caricature. He is clearly symbolic, since he serves as a witness to the concept and practice of revolutions past. We are told that he had been in Berlin during the uprisings of 1848 and in Paris during the commune of 1871, as well as now being in Denmark of the 1880s, "the very time that political tension and agitation had reached their height in the land."[1] When the little man talks to people about the past, he momentarily evokes their "urge for action" and "irrepressible courage

Political Parables

to fight and sacrifice" themselves to a "great and sacred cause, for liberty, justice, and fraternity."[2] There is a head-on collision between this representative of proletarian activism and the *de facto* leader of the village, the schoolmaster Zachariasen. Nominally a champion of the enlightenment as identified with the ideas of N. F. S. Grundtvig, Zachariasen represents the peaceful, almost quiescent and lethargic countryside and the status quo. The reader understands that the little man's position is extreme and his methods unacceptable and impractical if change is really to be effected in the village. Nevertheless, the reader is meant to sympathize with him and reject the pompousness and self-satisfaction of Zachariasen as a representative of the cautious rural community.

The only hope for real change seems to lie in those persons who have no vested interest in the established order—the rabble, to use the little man's term. Apparently only people who have nothing to lose are willing to sacrifice themselves for an ideal; the average bourgeois is so concerned with the chase after security and the desire to reproduce his own world once more in his children that there is little hope for any fundamental alteration or the alleviation of conditions which, all critical minds will admit, are in need of improvement.

Within his narrative, Pontoppidan brings the argument to a head by depicting a public meeting where the villagers are to vote upon an address that is to be sent to the king. The message contains a veiled warning of a possible uprising if conditions in the country do not take a turn for the better. The effort is so timid, however, that it is doomed to failure from the start. The villagers do not recognize the wordiness of their village Caesar, the teacher Zachariasen, for what it is and are impressed by his bloated rhetoric. The little man attempts by the use of irony to show the villagers how ridiculous their petty effort is, but is shouted down after he suggests that three ludicrous village characters, instead of three stout farmers, should transmit the address to the king, that the address should be given an appropriate calligraphic form and be bound in goat's leather, and, finally, that there three cheers be given for the monarch. The total incomprehension of his remarks by the villagers is a crushing blow, and the little man who, some years ago, had appeared from nowhere in the village, packs his few belongings and sets out into the unknown once more. The narrator meets him at the top of Gallows Hill as he is leaving. The little man finally has an interested audience of one to listen to his forthright criticism of the social order, his championing of the concept of freedom, and his principle that freedom can be preserved only by sacrifice.

"Gallows Hill at Ilum" had an interesting genesis. It was first published in 1889 as a series of letters to a Danish newspaper (*Københavns Børstidende*) to which Pontoppidan was a regular contributor under the pseudonym "Urbanus."[3] The letter form was abandoned for subsequent publication, and Pontoppidan also undertook numerous changes in diction and phrasing. As he did with practically all his works, he subsequently revised the stories in *Skyer* and altered the language. While it is apparent that Pontoppidan was anxious to change his style for self-satisfaction, it is not always easy for the reader to see any compelling motivation for the change. The phrase "gendarme-blue sea" remains in all versions of the story, however; it is a key to the historicity of the narrative. In the first version Pontoppidan is sarcastic regarding the position of the churches in the landscape, but he does not yet describe them as cackling hens. Here the churches are ringing their bells and in competition with one another "just like white roosters that crow to one another each from his manure pile." The original formulation must be said to be considerably less subtle than the final one. The criticism of Grundtvigianism is sharper in the first version, where Pontoppidan writes "at all times and everywhere there were lectures. Where five people had assembled, the four of them felt obliged to 'cite an old phrase' or 'tell a little folktale.'"[4] The contrast between dream and reality, between boast and action is castigated in particular in the sentence, "And the bloodiest accomplishments of their forefathers are ever the reason for their enthusiasm."

The beginning of "Ilum Galgebakke" can be quoted as an example of Pontoppidan's irony and his ability to achieve a desired effect. There are many parallels in Pontoppidan's work to the beginning of "Ilum Galgebakke" with its apparent idyll, shattered by Pontoppidan's parenthetical comments, that provide a contrast to the action in the story. The story begins:

Just outside the village of Ilum lies the so-called Gallows Hill. To climb it, you go up a narrow path which winds its way between ploughed fields and young plantations of spruce and pine. With every upward step you take, the panorama opens about you, and when at last you reach the bald summit of the hill, the whole district lies spread out before you for miles around. On three sides, it is surrounded by that ancient guardian of the land—the gendarme-blue sea, whose armies of waves can be discerned in the distance.

The phrase "gendarme-blue sea" was identified above as the key to the irony of the story. The blue referred to was the color of the uniforms of the federal police, the gendarmerie sent out from Copenhagen to enforce the decrees of the provisional government. To Pontoppidan's contemporaries, the allusion was unmistakable. The combination of idyll and irony is continued in the third paragraph which begins: "If you go up there on a quiet summer evening when the setting sun is spreading a sheen of melted butter over every puddle and ditch, when the churches on the hills around are beginning to cluck like white hens...." The equation of clucking white hens and village churches is typical for Pontoppidan's irreverent attitude toward the status quo and the established church.

What is told in a nominally matter-of-fact way about the violence enacted between estate owners and peasants of Ilum in the past is no less than bloodcurdling, and suggests a justification for the use of force to obtain human rights. But now the struggle for independence has assumed "more civilized forms" which in turn means that the common man has lost his rights. Pontoppidan makes this point almost with a sigh. The times of bold action are long past. He has nevertheless insinuated an idea into the reader's mind; the suggestion will be reinforced when the grotesque little man dares speak for revolutionary action. The reader is not totally unprepared for such a position.

The irony and the sarcasm with which Pontoppidan's words are charged are veiled by his dignified, almost stately manner of description, his measured sentences and subdued, although cutting, metaphors. The use of dialogue is limited. Unlike

Herman Bang, whose strength lies in letting the reader deduce events from conversation that is often trivial in itself, Pontoppidan makes no use of small talk. As a narrator he is a traditionalist: omniscient and sometimes projecting himself into the narrative. He uses direct speech to make dramatic situations come alive, to indicate a change of pace or an intensity of emotion in the story.

The dissension that political tension during the years of the provisional government could engender is more directly illustrated in the story "To Venner" ("Two Friends"). The friends' previous ability to complement one another through their very differences of opinion and character is undermined by the fury of conviction that has grasped each man, one a clergyman, the other an auditor. This particular story suggests the erosion of a *modus vivendi* and of personal mutual respect simply because of differences regarding the actions and intent of the current government. The lack of tolerance seems to the reader to be more objectionable than the principles of either party.

In another story, "To Gange mødt" ("Twice Met") Pontoppidan writes with pathos about a would-be revolutionary who has lived in self-imposed exile in Norway for years in order to return to Copenhagen at the critical moment. Misled into believing that that moment has come, he returns to Copenhagen only to discover that the leaders of his "liberal" party are but self-satisfied patriotic bourgeois. A similar motif is found in "Et Offer" ("Sacrifice") in which a shoemaker with political ambitions compromises himself by declaring for the conservative party and letting himself be exploited for the sake of a momentary and illusory notoriety. He succeeds only in destroying his own business; the proletarians no longer want their shoes repaired by a traitor to their cause and the well-to-do have no need of his services. Disappointed and under great duress he loses command of reason. When, as a result, he is incarcerated, his family is sent to the poorhouse, his wife solaced by an offcial who assures her that she will be better off there than she had been for a long time.

Satirical but lighthearted is the brief tale "Den første Gendarm" ("The First Gendarme"), in which the honor of a village is saved by a small barking dog. He accomplishes by chance

Political Parables

what the villagers had sworn to do but, when the proper moment presented itself, had reneged. The gendarmes, whose existence had been suggested at the beginning of the "Gallows at Ilum Hill" by identifying the color of the sea with their uniforms, were unwelcome reminders of the oppressiveness of the state and its prime minister. The inhabitants of Pontoppidan's favorite village of his own invention, Lillelunde (the name means Littlewood), had sworn that the first gendarme who showed himself in their village would be subject to a demonstration that would signify their opposition to the prime minister. They had moreover agreed that the first gendarme who entered Lillelunde would not leave it unscathed.

When a gendarme finally does appear, the villagers are nonplussed, some by the dignity of his uniform, some by the quality of his mount, and some by his handsome moustache. At the crucial moment they neither act nor speak, and the gendarme rides on through the village, leaving reticent and shamefaced men behind him, as girls begin to titter. At this juncture a nondescript cur, the tailor's half-breed poodle, frightens the horse, which stumbles on a stone in the road and unsaddles his rider. The gendarme is thrown onto the dusty road and suffers a minor, superficial face wound. Now the men are free to laugh. Their threat has been carried out and their honor has, just barely, been saved.

The point of the tale is the same as that in "Gallows Hill at Ilum" but it seems more abstract and less bitter in its denunciation of the twin lacks of effective leadership and ability to organize to change the established order. It is a variation on a theme: weakness born of inaction and the lack of civil courage.

The "Clouds" to which the title of Pontoppidan's book alludes are storm clouds, or at least clouds that obliterate the sunlight. Once more, Pontoppidan is insinuating that enlightenment is necessary for the well-being of the commonweal, an enlightenment coupled with self-understanding and courage. The mood of the stories, taken together, is not simple. On the one hand, Pontoppidan holds a distorting mirror up to his countrymen so that they can see the grotesque and objectionable political conditions under which they have been living. His own convictions and position are unmistakable and are clearly meant to be inculcated into the reader. On the other hand, he is suggesting that the inertia of the petit bourgeoisie or the average citizen is probably too great to be overcome. A lack of will, reinforced by a fear of the consequences of change and the selfishness of most individuals when their own possessions or the future of their children might be at stake, will result in the continued exploitation of the mass of the population by clever politicians who understand how to employ the metaphors of God and country to their own advantage.

At first glance the reader might assume that the Pontoppidan of *Skyer* was a revolutionary, but the true revolutionary enjoys the optimistic conviction that radical change will produce an ideal new society and that the weaknesses from which any given society suffers can be eradicated by a change of political regimes. Ultimately, however, the reader understands that Pontoppidan is not optimistic. Even the little man at Gallows Hill at Ilum harbors little optimism and implies that the achievement of a more intelligently governed society is a long-term process, not necessarily encouraged or even desired by the governed.

Pontoppidan harbors more silent rage than hope. While able to represent both acidly and humorously conditions which are not ideal, he suggests that the major flaw is not the arbitrary nature of social organization but rather the lack of real character within most human breasts. He is by no means nihilistic: he does not reject all extant values and he does not intimate that the political entity of Denmark should be exchanged for some other. The virtues of sincerity and frugality, of lucidity and altruism are suggested in a mood of admiration and appreciation. Moreover, there is an awareness of the natural beauties of the landscape and the inherent goodness of a life not too far removed from the natural order of the nonhuman world. He understands dedication to craftsmanship and to ideals of human endeavor not guided solely by the profit motive, and believes self-cognition to be the greatest good.

For the reader who already knows something of Pontoppidan's later production, a link connects the philosophy that informs *Skyer* and the earlier stories with the later narrative works, particularly Pontoppidan's best-known and most widely read book, the novel of development, *Lykke-Per*, which began to appear only eight years after *Skyer* had been published. There can be no understanding of what is wrong with society, Pontoppidan suggests, until the individual looks deep into himself and gains a modicum of objectivity toward his own motivations and, consequently, his own actions. *Lykke-Per*, to be sure, will furnish no suggestion as to how society as a whole might be improved. The early attempts by the title character of that novel to change society are seen to be generated solely from personal ambition, with a ruthless disregard for the real needs of one's fellow men. *Lykke-Per*, however, does depict one way for the individual to achieve peace of mind and intimates that any sweeping social change should begin with the individual. The real revolution must be won within the mind of each human being and not be superimposed by an outside force driven by ulterior motives. As long as the characters in the stories of *Skyer* remain as they are, without having gained greater self-understanding and without having accepted their own part of the responsibility for social, political, or economic conditions to which they object in the abstract, there can be no fundamental and lasting improvement.

Pontoppidan's bent, then, is more philosophical than political. One is consequently not surprised to learn that he never was active politically, never allied himself with any political party, and never participated in efforts to gain some particular reform. One is reminded of Henrik Ibsen who time and again was looked upon by his contemporaries as the champion of certain reforms, such as women's rights, but who at the height of his career declared flatly that he did not hold with any special reforms; what needed to be reformed was the human being. There is, one might note, not a little of Peer Gynt in Pontoppidan's Per Sidenius (in *Lykke-Per*). The narrow views of most of the characters who people *Skyer* parallel the views of many of Ibsen's characters in the later plays, whose basic flaw is a lack of cognition and who are loathe to alter a social order that Ibsen shows us to be warped, insincere, and selfish.

CHAPTER 6

Patriotic Interludes

I Reisebilder aus Dänemark

CLOSELY related but nevertheless in contrast to Pontoppidan's early imaginative works in which he pictured Danish country life is the small book he wrote at the request of the Danish Tourist Association for publication in German: *Reisebilder aus Dänemark* (1890). Pontoppidan wrote no ordinary travel book, if only because he was a creative writer close to the soil, more concerned with depicting landscape than urban life. German readers must have received an unusual impression of Denmark. Little more than 4 of the book's 106 pages are devoted to the Danish capital, perhaps because, as Pontoppidan himself notes, any satisfactory introduction to Copenhagen would require a separate volume. He would scarcely have been the person to write such a volume, since his orientation was not metropolitan.

Pontoppidan writes as a patriot in the older sense of the word: a man who loves his country, but without any political bone to pick. He is not a chauvinist. He waxes poetic in defining Denmark as "a child of the sea, a foster-son of the waves from whose womb it slowly arose in the morning of time." He is appreciative of the fact that, despite its small size, Denmark offers much variety. Pontoppidan's predilection for landscapes serves him in good stead. In many of his stories, the landscapes, as we already have observed, play a major role in setting the mood of the narrative and suggesting the action that is to follow. In *Reisebilder*, Pontoppidan could give himself wholly over to the description of landscape without the need to use it as a device, and he does so from both a historical and modern perspective. While Pontoppidan is discussing what a contemporary

Patriotic Interludes 55

viewer might see, he has an eye to the past from which the genesis of the present can be deduced.

Pontoppidan's enthusiasm for his subject is striking. Sea and shore, sunsets and beech woods, lakes and cliffs: all these can evoke in him an appreciative warmth. The permutations of the natural world command Pontoppidan's attention. He devotes few words to people and customs and says next to nothing about commerce, agriculture, and industry. Pontoppidan indicates that the individual must find himself in the landscape and sense the elements which are the ultimate determining factors of life in Denmark. He does pay attention to fishing and shipping, the traditional occupations of the country. In particular he describes the North Sea coast and its annual shipwrecks. Pontoppidan lets the leader of a lifesaving group tell of a recent tragic shipwreck.

That Pontoppidan is especially favorably disposed to the Jutland peninsula is not surprising, for he was a native of Jutland. The area around Silkeborg in central Jutland he identifies as "a Danish paradise" of idyllic beauty and "fairy tale magnificence that overwhelms the senses." But he is similarly affected by the landscape of the island of Funen: "It is all an unsurpassed panorama, although it is but the head of a pin on the map."

Toward the end of the book Pontoppidan does allude to some of the monumental buildings of the capital, above all the renaissance edifices constructed in the seventeenth century during the reign of Christian IV, such as Rosenborg Castle and the Exchange (but also the castle at Frederiksborg at Hillerød, some miles outside the capital). Pontoppidan describes the island of Zealand as offering "rest and recreation" because of its friendly landscape. Somewhat incongruously, the book ends with a suggestion that the visitor travel to Roskilde to see the medieval cathedral in which most of the Danish monarchs have been buried since the late Middle Ages. Pontoppidan, who was neither a good monarchist nor a good churchman, nevertheless calls the cathedral Denmark's "proudest national monument."

Pontoppidan's Denmark is attractive but somewhat grim. The demands of daily life on land and at sea outweigh the idyllic, but an impression of natural strength and dignity is conveyed to the reader. There is no suggestion either of the sophisticated or luxurious life of the Copenhagen patrician or of the rising social democracy which was to shape Denmark's daily life in years to come.

II *Two Miniatures*

Hidden in a monumental, charming, but now nearly forgotten topographical work, published between 1887 and 1893, are two lengthy articles by Pontoppidan about life and landscape in part of Jutland and part of the island of Funen respectively. The work is the four-volume *Danmark*, edited by Martinus Galschiøt (1844–1940). The first volume was issued three years prior to Pontoppidan's *Reisebilder aus Dänemark*. Here one discovers the genesis of that book, for some bits of the narrative and description were translated and introduced into the German work. More important is the fact that Pontoppidan, nominally charged with producing introductions to parts of Denmark's topography, is in fact writing in a fashion strongly reminiscent of his own imaginative work. That the sketches of life in Jutland and on Funen resemble his pictures of social life in the volume *Fra Hytterne* is not surprising; it was also published in 1887.

The subtitle of Galschiøt's folios identifies them as containing "sketches and pictures by Danish authors and artists." Pontoppidan is in good company, for other contributors include such well-known Danes as the poet Holger Drachmann, the older and well-established novelists Vilhelm Bergsøe (1835–1911), Sophus Schandorph, and Zacharias Nielsen (1844–1922), the folklorist Evald Tang Kristensen (1843–1929), the dialectologist H. F. Feilberg (1831–1921), and the journalist Edvard Brandes (1847–1931), as well as three other prominent younger writers: Sophus Bauditz (1850–1915), Karl Gjellerup, and Johannes Jørgensen (1866–1956). While most of these other writers can be said to have obediently produced contributions that might be labelled "description and travel," Pontoppidan remains the narrator most of the time. The beginning of the chapter on Randers, the scene of Pontoppidan's childhood, is masterful in suggesting the nature of life in a provincial Danish town through anecdotes. It reads as if it were a part of one of Pontoppidan's

Patriotic Interludes 57

original stories—for example, from *Fra Hytterne*. The style, clarity of imagery, diction, and humor might, to be sure, be mistaken for that of Meïr Goldschmidt, the Danish author with whom Pontoppidan has most frequently been compared.

While the other contributors properly addressed themselves to scenery, monuments, buildings, and sights, Pontoppidan was now concerned chiefly with the people, and particularly the small town characters who inhabit the landscape with its villages and towns. Pontoppidan shows himself sensitive to a changing social code, to the new replacing the old, to which he looked back with some amusement and only occasional nostalgia.

The details that Pontoppidan provides are evidence of incisive observation and personal experience. He had known or at least seen and heard many of the characters of whom he wrote; he had made the voyage on a storm-tossed steamer through the Kattegat; he had participated in the journeys which were the basis for his observations, although sometimes as a matter of course or even out of necessity, and not merely as a tourist or a journalist. He did not try to depict an idyll, but he was appreciative of the niceties and differences in the Danish land and seascape. Moreover, the kind of description which Pontoppidan furnishes is that made only by someone who knows the landscape well; one deduces that he must have traversed it by foot to be able to portray its nuances so thoroughly. Pontoppidan's strong literary bent is also recognizable. The chapter entitled "Between the Fjords" begins, "Landscapes are like books. If they are to be interesting they must be imbued with a grand and pervasive mood which overtakes one irresistably, ... the more powerfully, the more one penetrates the subject, or they must possess contrasting elements which each in its way is set off from what surrounds it...."[1]

That parts of Pontoppidan's descriptive passages found their way into *Reisebilder aus Dänemark* three years later is not unexpected, but it is surprising to find a section of the description of Funen in volume II of *Danmark* (1893) reappearing, in part word for word, in Pontoppidan's short novel *Den gamle Adam* (*The Old Adam*) the next year. The imaginative quality of the anecdote about a visit to a watering place on the west coast of Funen is so striking that it might well be that this particular section of the article on Funen originally had been written as a part of the narrative that later became *Den gamle Adam*, and not vice versa. Or perhaps what really was a personal experience a few years earlier was translated into fiction in 1894.

Not all of the chapter on west Funen is equally imaginative. In order to cover the geographic area, Pontoppidan does speak of castles and estates, but the overall impression of his introduction to Jutland and Funen is not to be equated to one derived from Baedeker. On the whole, he gives a fresh, original interpretation of the landscape and its inhabitants, and exudes warmth and enthusiasm, so that the reader feels encouraged to visit and see for himself those places Pontoppidan describes. No wonder, then, that the Danish Tourist Association engaged Pontoppidan to write *Reisebilder*.

III A Winter Journey

Pontoppidan's patriotism and national pride found a curious late expression in the small volume *En Vinterrejse* (*A Winter Journey*, 1920). The book purports to be "leaves from a diary" kept on a trip to Norway some years before. It is indeed a piece of travel literature, although there is interwoven the motif of the author's searching for a young Dane who has left his family and his studies in Copenhagen and disappeared in Norway. How much is truth and how much poetry in *En Vinterrejse* it is not possible to judge accurately, but the opinions, rather strong and prejudiced, need not have been expressed were they not those of the author. There is simply no reason for having any fictional narrator-traveller make them. They reflect what Pontoppidan the traveller has seen and done in Norway and how he has reacted inwardly. Just when the trip to Norway was made is not specified, but toward the end of his stay there Pontoppidan heard a lecture by Bjørnstjerne Bjørnson—who died in 1910 at the age of 78. In the year of Bjørnson's death, Pontoppidan had published some preliminary sketches from the trip to Norway in a popular magazine, and he mentioned that he had left Copenhagen right after Christmas. Thus the journey must have taken place in January of 1909,

Patriotic Interludes

about the time that Pontoppidan began writing his five-volume *De Dødes Rige* (*The Realm of the Dead*, 1912–16).

Particularly striking in the observations made in Norway is the tendency to measure everything against conditions in Denmark, which serves as the model and exemplar. Pontoppidan, otherwise known as the great chastiser of his countrymen, suddenly resembles the tourist who finds everything better at home when he is abroad. He is ironically critical of the Norwegians in general but also of the Lapps, toward whom he seems to harbor little sympathy. Let a single example suffice: "As everywhere in Norway, the farms lie far from one another, not as with us in pleasant villages.... Many of the huts of day laborers can only be compared with our most miserable pigsties."[2] Pontoppidan tires of the grandiose mountain landscape and concludes that "An ordinary Danish roadside gives to the pious viewer a more intimate and more heartfelt relationship with nature than all the marvels of nature" in Norway.[3] To most, Pontoppidan's attitude will seem oddly parochial and narrow.

Like many Danes, Pontoppidan senses the ridiculous in Norwegian chauvinism, notably the reaction against much that was Danish after several centuries of Danish sovereignty. In a spirit which we know from his other works, Pontoppidan intimates that the Lutheran state church is the one place where the Norwegians might best have started a national reform: yet the clergyman he meets on the bitterly cold and windy street in northerly Hammerfest wears the ruff and stovepipe hat of his Danish brother of the cloth who functions in a less frigid climate.

Pontoppidan had fled Copenhagen grumbling about the culinary excesses of the Christmas holidays. His experience in Norway was different from life in the Danish capital, and it evoked a different kind of social satire and criticism on his part. Neither the people nor the landscape provided an ideal which might have served to keep him away from Denmark for any length of time. In fact, the Norwegian sojourn furnished a contrast which made the return to his homeland the more agreeable. Pontoppidan shows himself to be something of a Sidenius, his own symbolic creation for the traditional Danish bourgeois, after all. He "understands the disappointments" of the young man whose track he is following, but lacks comprehension for the lasting attraction of the mountains, of desolation, wilderness, and solitude. Yet Pontoppidan's alter ego, Per Sidenius ("Lykke Per") finally was to find himself only when he withdrew from society and sought desolation and solitude.

CHAPTER 7

The Kingdom Comes Not

I *The Dream*

THE first of the three multi-volume works by Henrik Pontoppidan which *inter alia* furnish a broad canvas of Denmark between 1880 and 1910 is *Det forjættede Land* (*The Promised Land*), originally issued in three parts, 1891–95. Volume I, *Muld* (*Sod*), volume II, *Det forjættede Land* (*The Promised Land*), and volume III, *Dommens Dag* (*The Day of Judgment*) each bears the subtitle "A Picture of the Times." The books do indeed depict conditions of daily life around 1880 in Denmark. The picture is, however, a critical one; Pontoppidan has frequently and for good reason been called the castigator of Denmark. As in some of his shorter, earlier works, he views numerous aspects of the established order with irony and makes apparent the need for various reforms. Not only are the authorities chastised, however, for time and again Pontoppidan lays bare commonplace weaknesses in human character. While the life of the Danish country dweller seems frequently to receive more admiration than that of his urban contemporary, his failings are equally visible and rural life is no ideal in Pontoppidan's narratives.

While one can deduce much about Danish society in the 1880s from *The Promised Land*, the volumes do not merely comprise a picture of the times. They constitute a psychological novel of development and change in the major character, Emanuel Hansted, who begins as a conservative young clergyman, gradually undergoes a series of transformations, and ends as a madman.

After a lengthy description of a heavy snowstorm in rural Zealand, the narrator introduces the young Emanuel Hansted, fresh from theological training and ordination in Copenhagen, into the isolated but worldly rectory where he is to serve as the chaplain for the Rev. Mr. Tønnesen. The dean of a double parish on the island of Zealand, Tønnesen lives more in the fashion of the lord of the manor than of a priest and is in general quite out of touch with the times and at loggerheads with his parish. The Grundtvigian movement, represented in the parish by a weaver named Hansen who holds semireligious public meetings that are considerably more popular than Tønnesen's church services, is ultimately the cause for most dissension. The lines are clearly drawn: on the one hand Tønnesen and the established conservative church and on the other Hansen and popular awakening through the medium of Grundtvig's ideas and the folk-high-school movement.

At their first meeting, the conflict between church and parishioners is thrust upon Emanuel Hansted by his superior, who speaks at length of the sorry state of religious life in the community and the tensions which obtain. In his anger and concern about where it all will end, Dean Tonnesen works himself into a fury, to the young chaplain's distress and amazement. When the dean finally asks rhetorically whether Pastor Hansted wants their common endeavors to be for the glory of God and the benefit of the parish, Hansted can only reply in all honesty that he has no higher wish. The stage is set: the two men, although they may use the same terminology, fail to understand one another's motivations.

After a sudden confrontation with Hansen, Emanuel Hansted agrees to address one of the weaver's popular meetings. Speaking freely and with enthusiasm, he captivates his audience. As a result he soon finds himself in clear-cut opposition to his superior Tønnesen, in whose manse he is living. The reasons for Emanuel's change of heart are not merely theological or social. From his very first day in the parish, when he was sent out through the snowstorm to visit a sick person, he has been attracted to the patient, surprisingly enough an attractive young country girl who had spent a term at a local Danish folk-highschool. Emanuel declares himself to her the same evening he has spoken at Weaver Hansen's meeting and the next day their engagement is known throughout the parishes. This event causes a shock in the rectory, not only because it marks a total shift in political stance by Emanuel, but also because there had

The Kingdom Comes Not

been a tacit understanding that Emanuel might marry Tønnesen's daughter Ragnhild, a sophisticated and lonely beauty who found in Emanuel the only person in her rural solitude with whom she could really converse.

In his anger, Tønnesen requests that the ecclesiastical authorities remove Emanuel as his chaplain, but effects only his own removal. His unwilling adversary, Emanuel, is instated as his successor. Through his engagement and marriage, Emanuel establishes close ties to the rural community and assumes the role of a priest of the people. He finds that he is the more welcome there, because his mother, who later had grown demented and had finally taken her own life, had been looked upon as an angelic spirit of the same community in her early years. To the alert readers of the 1890s, who had been inculcated with the doctrine that heredity and milieu are major forces in life which should be reflected in literature, the mention of the mother's fate suggested what was eventually in store for the son.

In this first volume of *The Promised Land,* Pontoppidan demonstrates himself to be a master of the naturalistic sketch. The characters which he describes are real and convincing in their actions and motivations. The situations—sometimes ironic, sometimes satirical—in which the persons of the book find themselves are memorable. Although they do not always contribute to the forward motion of the narrative, they are parts of the general mosaic.

Pontoppidan's preoccupation with description, both establishing the mood of a narrative and introducing the setting to the reader, is manifested at the beginning of *Muld.* He devotes the first four small pages in the original version of the book to a detailed depiction of landscape and snowstorm, after he announced in a preliminary one-sentence paragraph (deleted in later editions) that "It was a year toward the end of the seventies." This sentence proclaims the author's intent to portray events and conditions at a given time—that is, only a dozen or so years previously. The later omission of this significant statement suggests Pontoppidan's desire to imbue his work with greater temporal validity and to avoid having it looked upon primarily as a period piece.

Stark images of a storm follow: it had raged for eight days;

it had come on the "blue-black wings of clouds chasing from the east...."[1] In his revision, Pontoppidan substituted "several" for "eight," and let the clouds come "flying" rather than "chasing" from the east. In the altered version he is not only less specific, but less hyperbolic. This is characteristic of his revisions. On second thought, on reflection, he leaves more to the imagination of the reader and employs less dramatic metaphor. The images which seemed to him essential do remain. In both editions he mentions "fallen trees, broken telegraph poles, burst seed ricks, and dead birds which the hurricane had struck down to earth and killed instantly."[2] Although the background is rural, it is not idyllic as the story begins—or, if there is an idyll, there are forces which could disrupt it. Moreover, the storm is not without metaphysical and allegorical significance, for, we are told, there were people dwelling in the sorely afflicted landscape who quietly began "to search their own consciences and make their peace with God in a belief that the Day of Judgment was nigh."[3] Perhaps, yes, perhaps all this was a warning, "a divine prophecy of some significant happening which in the near future would overtake the town or the parish or perhaps the entire country."[4] The reader senses impending significant change, the likelihood that something will overtake and possibly disrupt town and parish.

The next sentence, beginning the second chapter of the first of *Muld*'s five books, introduces the unwitting agent of change: "In the dean's study this evening there sat a young stranger who the day before had arrived during the wildest raging of the snowstorm."[5] A careful delineation of the young man follows, but not until a page later is he identified as the dean's new chaplain. Only after an additional page is the chaplain's name, and then but the family name, revealed: Pastor Hansted.

It is typical of Pontoppidan's narrative technique that he describes a person or place at length before providing the reader with an identification by name. The reader is therefore forced to be the more attentive, since he must discover who the person is about whom he has been furnished such a catalogue of circumstantial details. By so doing, Pontoppidan increases suspense. He also provides a key to the background and character of the person being introduced, much as a dramatist like

The Kingdom Comes Not

Ibsen, who, through stage directions, gives rich hints about the telling qualities of those persons about to carry out the action upon the stage. Because of the vagaries of styles in clothing, Pontoppidan's descriptions no longer speak as unequivocally as they originally did, but there is essential information couched in the graphic language: "He was a tall, slightly built figure in long, black clothes and with a white necktie at his throat. From a pale and childish face stared a pair of extremely pale blue eyes with a frank expression. Above his forehead, which was high and convexly arched, handsome blond hair flowed, slightly curled at the ends...."[6] This is no self-possessed man of the world sitting across from the reverend dean (who, we soon discover, is physically the chaplain's antithesis). The dean is a strongly built man with a large head and heavy, short white hair. His black eyebrows partly conceal his dark grey eyes, while his prominent nose and full lips give him almost a Mediterranean appearance. He is beardless whereas the chaplain has fuzz, if not yet real whiskers, on his cheeks and his chin. Moreover, the dean is dressed in worldly splendor, with a white scarf rather than a necktie, a silken vest, and highly polished boots.

Here indeed are opposites. We sense a differing philosophy of life and total incompatibility before a word has been exchanged between the two men. And it is almost exclusively the dean who speaks: "Dean Tønnesen had begun his lecture in a quiet, didactic tone...."[7] He warns Pastor Hansted against forces that are undermining the authority of the Church: those disastrous currents which in the name of the struggle for democratic freedom and equality have risen from the depths of the population and found their way into the sacred halls of the Church! Tønnesen's bombastic words confirm him as an opponent of democratic endeavor, something Pontoppidan had already subtly implied in describing his dress.

The care that Pontoppidan took with his diction, his utilization of aural as well as visual imagery, and his tendency toward effective alliteration in prose can only be recognized in the original Danish text. Even without a knowledge of Danish, however, the reader can observe the repetition of sound in Pontoppidan's third (later second) sentence: "Paa vildt forrevne, sorteblaa Skyvinger var Stormen kommen jagende fra Øst og havde gennempisket Fjorden, saa store Skumflager var kastet højt op paa Markerne."[8] The repetition of the sound "v" in the combination "vildt Forrevne" may be unintentional, although the suggestion of violence which the phrase evokes is intentional; this particular combination of words is far from usual. The "s" alliteration of "Sorteblaa Skyvinger...Stormen...saa store Skumflager" is scarcely chance; Pontoppidan is, after all, also trying aurally to evoke the image of a severe and strident snowstorm. To stress Pontoppidan's repetition of sounds would be misleading, however. He uses the device only upon occasion—it would otherwise be intolerable. He is far more exacting in the matter of diction and in the articulation of those scenes and images which can correspond to the images and other narrative elements engendered in his own mind.

Although there is much description in Pontoppidan's narrative, his prose is easy to read, chiefly because he generally employs short sentences. The sentences vary from a few words to several lines, but they are never so involuted or lengthy that the reader loses his way or has to go back to reread a sentence or paragraph to be certain of the author's meaning. While Pontoppidan's images can be unusual and his speech metaphoric, his means of expression remain clear as crystal. For this very reason he is identified as the master of classical Danish prose. His dissatisfaction with what he wrote and the constant urge to rewrite is only further evidence of his attempt to be precise and clear.

Descriptive passages alternate with dialogue here as elsewhere in Pontoppidan. Sometimes the one kind of writing predominates, sometimes the other, although the narrative passages in which the author tells us about people and places, about human relations and events of either an everyday or catastrophic nature, far outweigh the dialogue. The dialogue is syntactically simple enough to be close to daily speech without reproducing either its triviality or its confusion and inaccuracy, and bridges the yawning gap which ordinarily separates written from oral language. This fact distinguishes Pontoppidan as a stylist from a still greater and more original artist, his contemporary Herman Bang. Pontoppidan does make

The Kingdom Comes Not

an effort to give some of the characters particular speech patterns, but any striking idiosyncracies of speech, notably the use of dialect, are confined to minor characters whose function is either to introduce a slight element of humor into the story or to suggest the unpolished ways of country folk. Occasionally there is a lyrical intercalation, but most often it has ironic intent. Thus, in "Gallows Hill at Ilum," the assembled villagers sing some of Grundtvig's most aggressively patriotic lines that should be a prelude to commitment and action—and do nothing. In this first volume of the trilogy Pontoppidan introduces a ballad from the Grundtvigian school at Sandinge to provide a contrast both to the accepted hymns of the established church and to Emanuel's own youthful experiences.

II *False Promise*

In the second volume, which carries the title later given the entire trilogy, *Det forjættede Land* (*The Promised Land*, 1892), Emanuel Hansted has established himself as a peasant clergyman and he attempts to realize the somewhat fantastic ideals which had motivated him at the end of volume I. Seven years have passed and Emanuel and his wife Hansine now have three children. The rectory is opened to the parishioners, who are welcome to drop in whenever they wish, who are never turned away if they are hungry, and who enjoy a close relationship with their pastor. Emanuel's dream of a rural idyll is nevertheless in vain and ends tragically. Unwilling to admit that his son could be suffering from a serious illness because of the sporadic nature of the symptoms from which the boy suffers, Emanuel refuses to let a physician treat the son until it is too late. The stark reality which is injected into his life by the death of his first born suggests the new tangent that his existence now takes. The passages dealing with the sickness of the child, the foolish optimism of the father, the antithetical attitudes of the two parents toward the illness and, in particular, the approaching death of the little boy, are touchingly realistic. They suggest observations made under duress and not merely a writer's imagination. One cannot help wondering how much autobiographical element is incorporated into the narrative, for Pontoppidan and his first wife, also an ill-matched pair, had lost their first child too.

In part because some of his public utterances are misunderstood, Emanuel gradually loses his hold on his parishioners. By chance, he again meets Ragnhild Tønnesen, who is visiting the local physician. After having cut himself off for a long time from the refined culture of Copenhagen which he had renounced, Emanuel lets himself partake for one evening of the social life of the doctor and his sophisticated urban friends. This experience gradually awakens within him an ineffable longing for the surroundings and society from which he sprang. His wife recognizes a change in her husband and is also able to divine its cause. When Emanuel has essentially reached the same position vis-à-vis his parishes that his predecessor had had, he confronts empty churches on Sunday and is not invited to meetings that pertain to matters of general importance for the community. He is now ready to accept defeat and to move elsewhere. His wife encourages him to seek a call in Copenhagen and Emanuel's move to the capital is ultimately effected. The promised land that he had sought and seemed to win has now slipped out of his grasp. The family bliss which he thought would be lasting has also disintegrated. His wife stays behind when Emanuel and their two daughters leave for Copenhagen. The union of the idealistic young clergyman and his peasant bride has been a failure, in part because, as we are told, Emanuel had the habit of most people "who, used to talking themselves, generally overhear remarks made by others."[9] Weaver Hansen rises up at the end of volume II after a long quiescence, and once more gains a hold over the residents of Vejlby.

Det forjættede Land is not just the story of Emanuel and Hansine Hansted. There are several threads interwoven in this second volume of the trilogy. The various levels of rural society in the parish of Vejlby are depicted and cleverly meshed in the story, so that their introduction seems reasonable to the reader. The contradictory political attitudes of the time find expression, as does also the political unrest of Denmark in the 1880s during the time of the provisional government which, as we learned from our examination of *Skyer*, was governed by ministerial decree rather than by laws made by the elected

The Kingdom Comes Not

members of parliament. There are also casual references to Sandinge Parish, the subject of Pontoppidan's first novel. We sense a unity of purpose in his writing by his connecting the early novel with the trilogy through the figure of Mrs. Gylling, who, in the later work, is mentioned as still holding her salon in Copenhagen. In this second volume, as in the previous one of the trilogy, Pontoppidan's technique is to present a series of interconnected but not necessarily interdependent situations that give a credible picture of a rural Danish community of the 1880s.

Thus the first paragraph of the second volume begins, "A man was plowing over on the broad acres north of Vejlby. He was a younger, tall figure in a patched smock made of sackcloth, with red wristlets above each hand and clumsy top boots from which the straps stuck out on both sides of the trousers' baggy knees."[10] The description continues for several lines, to be followed by a paragraph devoted to the image of the man and horse plowing while crows are hovering above. The reader assumes that the figure must be that of Emanuel Hansted, but is not certain until the third paragraph, where Emanuel is now identified, not merely as the pastor of the Vejlby and Skibberup parishes, but as " 'the modern apostle,' as some less kindly disposed colleagues in neighboring parishes were used pointedly to calling him."[11]

The description of Emanuel is now so different and in such contrast to the figure to whom the reader was introduced in the first volume of the trilogy that there is reason for some uncertainty. Not only Emanuel's dress but his physical appearance has changed radically. The fuzz on the cheeks of the young chaplain has been replaced by a long blond beard, so long that the wind blows it over one shoulder. "His face was emaciated, the forehead narrow and deeply sunken at the temples, the eyes were large, pale, gentle."[12] Pontoppidan had apparently given Emanuel's face the precise appearance he wished, for this description remained unchanged in later editions, although some deails of his outward appearance and of the landscape were altered, without noticeable effect. The broad acres became "high" acres and Emanuel's figure was no longer identified as "younger" while the "patched" smock was exchanged for a "coarse" one. That is, here as in the changes made when Emanuel was introduced in the first volume, Pontoppidan dampens his descriptive adjectives perceptibly and tends to be somewhat less dramatic.

III Doomsday

The final volume of the trilogy is *Dommens Dag* (*Judgment Day*, 1896). It distinguishes itself both in content and form from the first two volumes. On the one hand it provides a more pointed description of Emanuel Hansted's fate; on the other it is more consciously a "picture of the times" than either *Muld* or *Det forjættede Land*. A large part of the narrative is devoted to the popular religious gathering at Sandhinge folk-high-school—both the preparations and the meeting itself. While the first two volumes of the trilogy focus on the fate of one man, his ideal, his dream, and his ineffectiveness—in short, about problems which can be felt to have a direct or indirect relationship to the experiences of any reader in Western society—this third volume is much more a reflection of life in Denmark in the 1880s. Perhaps for this reason the English translation of *Det forjættede Land*, which appeared in 1896, comprised only the first two volumes of the trilogy: an English-speaking audience could not be expected to be familiar either with the role of the folk-high-school in Danish society or the theological questions which were debated there.

A case can, in fact, be made for the first two volumes constituting an independent narrative unit. The third volume is sufficiently different with regard both to Emanuel Hansted's fate and the technique of the narration itself that it can be considered unessential to the basic story, although scarcely capable of existing without the two preceding volumes. The rise and fall of action in *Muld* and *Det forjættede Land* makes independent consideration of these volumes defensible. The major character has tried and failed: he left the culture of the city and endeavored to become one with the rural population while attempting to be a servant of the word of God. His disillusionment leads to a cyclic conclusion in that he is reunited with his Copenhagen antecedents. The subsequent

The Kingdom Comes Not

return to Vejlby and Skibberup, the very parishes where he had failed to realize his dreams as a clergyman, is certainly unexpected and not wholly well-founded within Pontoppidan's story. Whether Mrs. E. V. Lucas, who translated the first two volumes of the trilogy into English[13] thought this way, or whether there were merely mundane economic reasons that decided against translating the third volume, we cannot know.

The inexorable fate of Emanuel Hansted can nevertheless be distinguished within the context of the entire narrative and interpreted as the resultant of the various destructive forces which were released previously. Uncertain of himself, but driven by a desire to serve what he interprets to be the will of God, Emanuel returns to the country and lives not far from the community where he earlier was a clergyman. There is no reunion with his wife; his widowed sister takes charge of the children and the household. Emanuel refuses to consider applying for a new parish without, however, establishing any organized plan of activity. He spends considerable time wandering about the countryside bringing the word of God to the simple, the impoverished, and the outcast of society. The efforts of older friends from Copenhagen and ecclesiastical superiors to make him face reality and appreciate the beauties of life and nature he looks upon as temptations of Satan. He becomes more and more the visionary who would reject this world for the kingdom of God. He speaks as a prophet, gradually identifying himself more and more as a Saviour. Among many simple folk he is held in reverence, but the consensus is that he is mentally unbalanced, as he finally demonstrates when he rises to address the large public meeting at the folk-high-school in Sandinge. After imploring God to speak through him, he falls silent, then to collapse after uttering "Lord, Lord, why hast Thou forsaken me?"[14] He subsequently believes that he has experienced Christ's passion and crucifixion; he is found raving mad on the heath. Even before his death, a down-to-earth clergyman who has several times attempted to draw Emanuel back into the routine of daily life coined an epitaph for him: "Here lies Don Quixote's ghost, Emanuel Hansted by name, who was born to be a good chaplain, but thought himself a prophet and a saint; who therefore took on the costume of a shepherd and felt every inspiration to be a special call from Heaven; who bungled everything that came into his hands, left his wife, and mistreated his children; but who nevertheless felt himself chosen by Providence to prepare the second coming and to preach God's judgment upon man."[15] Emanuel leaves behind a curious legacy, a little sect which looks upon him as "God's lamb" and cultivates his memory, as legends arise about his birth, his childhood, and the miracles he is supposed to have performed.

Viewed from the standpoint of narrative technique, *Dommens Dag* is more dramatic than the preceding volumes. Sections of the book contain philosophical discussions carried on by characters other than Emanuel and are only tangentially related to him. The impression left upon the reader is of an uncharacteristic preponderance of dialogue. The persons in the story are now characterized more by their verbal expression than by their outward appearance and actions, although, to be sure, appearances as well as actions continue to be important. What the reader has had to deduce in the earlier two volumes is more likely to be articulated by various characters. In the case of Emanuel Hansted, the explicit failure to be articulate is a characterization and at the same time a judgment, if not condemnation, of his "mission."

Not only is the name of the parish taken from Pontoppidan's first novel, *Sandinge Menighed*, but there are also other interconnections with the earlier novel, especially in the third volume of the trilogy. For example, the hypocritical Mrs. Gylling, who regularly pays lip service to the ideas of Grundtvig in *Sandinge Menighed*, now plays the role of hostess for the gathering at Sandinge folk-high-school.

There are also numerous autobiographical elements in *Det forjættede Land*. Pontoppidan was, of course, no dreamer like Emanuel Hansted. He did, however, at one time have an association with the folk-high-school movement and, more important, he did marry a country girl who was, so to speak, a product of the folk-high-school movement. Numerous situations in which he puts Emanuel and his wife were apparently drawn from personal experience, including the death of a first child. The reasons for the break up of Emanuel Hansted's marriage were ultimately the same as those that caused the break up of

The Kingdom Comes Not

Pontoppidan's marriage about the time the book was written, and the book has an introspective quality as far as the author himself is concerned.

We have alluded to the novel as giving insight into the Denmark, notably rural Denmark, of the 1880s, but in view of the fact that Pontoppidan gave each of the three volumes in the trilogy the subtitle "A Picture of the Times," we are warranted in asking how and in what way these novels do indeed constitute a picture of the times. One might assume that it was Pontoppidan's primary goal not to relate the story of a major character but rather to use him as a central figure who would permit passage from one stratum of society or one part of the country to the other. While it is conceivable that Pontoppidan originally may have had such a narrative device in mind, and retained a suggestion of that intent in the subtitle, the novel addresses itself more to the fate of one man and his struggle to establish a *modus vivendi* than to the portraiture of contemporary society. Nevertheless, the novel is a picture of the times.

In the first place, Pontoppidan describes daily life in rural Zealand in a more credible way than in the earlier stories, which tended to caricature and exaggerate. One senses that the author knew first-hand and intimately the kind of rural folk with whom he populates *Det forjættede Land*. The way his characters act and speak is naturalistic. The reader who has experienced rural life himself has the satisfaction of recognizing the familiar and can accept Pontoppidan's descriptions as a realistic portrayal. Even the reader whose orientation is wholly urban can comprehend that what he is reading corresponds to the observations that he has been able to make of the countryside and its dwellers. There is allusion to the current concerns of farmers, to an influx of new ideas about crops and machines, and even to the hard and isolated life of a fishing community.

In the second place, Pontoppidan is suggesting the continuing tension between urban and rural Danes and the gap which separates the internationally oriented, more modern inhabitants of the Danish capital, sophisticated and intellectual, and the nationally oriented, practical, and conservative villager who does not have an opportunity to ply or enjoy the arts or to engage in spirited social intercourse. Of this, the rural Dane has but an inkling derived from observation of those professionals—the clergyman, the doctor—whose fount of knowledge and place of training, if not of familial origin, is Copenhagen.

In the third place, Pontoppidan shows us the church foundering. Far from being united in a compatible Christian faith within the state church, the servants of the church are on the one hand either conservatively ineffective and self-serving willing subjects of the crown whose decorations are indicative of their submissiveness and their platitudes rather than any spiritual strength and originality, or, on the other hand, God-seekers who tend toward fanaticism and who act as divisive elements among those who would believe in the mystical body of Christ.

In the fourth place, by a kind of reflex action, the state seems as inanimate as the Church—which is an arm of the state. Not that the state founders; on the contrary—but the state gives no evidence of dynamism, but rather only of superannuation if not also of lethargy.

In the fifth place, Pontoppidan makes much of the Grundtvigian movement and in particular the role of the folk-high-school for the rural population. We know that he is writing not only on the basis of personal observation, but to some small extent at least, on the basis of a personal commitment. Pontoppidan senses and communicates the enthusiasms which gave the folk-high-schools their strength at the end of the nineteenth century. What the church and the state were unable to provide in the way of mental stimulus and a unifying belief in Denmark's present and future was suggested by the Grundtvigians, the happy Christians, who disseminated and shared both pride in Scandinavia's past and a faith in the possibility of a new community of believers in a new time. To be sure, Grundtvigianism was also in its way divisive both insofar as it was primarily a rural rather than an urban movement and insofar as it appealed neither to the conservative Danes who made up the backbone of the state church nor to the more serious minded, personally oriented pietists. Nevertheless, it was in the Grundtvigian movement that new stimulus and action were to be found. Since this was an important phenomenon in

Denmark at the time, it necessarily had to become part of any "picture of the times." If the ideas exuded by the folk-high-school in Pontoppidan's novel seem rather vague, it is because they *were* rather vague. What was important was that large numbers of people were brought together, as at the folk-high-school at Sandinge in Pontoppidan's first novel, for a kind of spiritual regeneration of a religio-socio-political nature—which is not to be equated with the proselytizing evangelism that made itself felt so strongly in the United States in the nineteenth century. Pontoppidan could not demonstrate what would come of the folk-high-school movement and its folk-meetings, for at his time of writing, the movement had not passed its zenith: it was there, it was a possibility for improvement, but one could scarcely prophesy more.

Finally, the novel portrays a society which, to a considerable extent, preserved the class system, yet did not connote any serious kind of stigma of caste. The well-to-do remain well-to-do and the poor remain poor without any threat to or promise of a change in their condition. Civil servants tend to reproduce civil servants, be they clergymen or judges, while maids and hired hands accept their lot as given without any suggestion of changing the social order. When Emanuel marries his Hansine, the community is somewhat taken aback, although also pleased, not only because a university-educated Copenhagener marries a country girl who has attended the folk-high-school, but also because a relatively affluent young man of the civil servant class is united with the daughter of a smallholder.

CHAPTER 8

Memoir and Pathos

THE short novels that Pontoppidan wrote while he was completing (and in one case probably after he had completed) *Det forjættede Land* are less easy to characterize than the early stories and novels that were imbued with social and political indignation, and are also very different among themselves. The earliest of these books, *Minder* (*Memories*, 1893), is a curious blend of memoir and melodramatic love story. The descriptions are in the spirit of *Reisebilder aus Dänemark* of three years before, and the reader senses that the author is writing about a town and countryside with which he is intimately familiar. That is, the "memories" are his own rather than those of the characters in the narrative. As a consequence, *Minder* impresses the reader as being less unified, as having less integrity, than most of the other short novels.

The small book has a certain charm in nostalgic descriptions that make up more than half of its pages. Its sentimental and unlikely love story is told in bits and pieces and assumes form only toward the end of the narrative. Almost one-third of the book is given over to an account of the author's return to the city of Randers (where Pontoppidan had spent his boyhood) and the many memories that the landscape, the sights, and the inhabitants evoke, coupled with detailed pictures of the town and its environs as they now exist. Pontoppidan gives great care to the wording of the imagery while at the same time seeking to portray realistically experiences and scenes with which any Dane who made the trip from Copenhagen to Randers might be familiar. For many pages there is no suggestion of the tragic story which is to be interwoven, at first casually, with the sentimental journey; the reader assumes that the journey and the childhood memories comprise the

Memoir and Pathos

actual content of the book. We first read of a rough nocturnal voyage through Kattegat on a small steamer. The resulting disorder and sea sickness are humorously pictured, but are then superseded as the steamer reaches its morning destinations. Quiet inland waters and fresh sea air dispel the night's unpleasantness. This experience repeated itself over and over again for travellers from Zealand to Jutland, who necessarily went by water until very recent decades—before rapid ferries, express trains, and giant bridges. As a consequence, Pontoppidan's descriptions appealed to the average Danish reader, who knew the very conditions that the author recreated, albeit more poignantly and articulately than the traveller himself could have done.

For all that, Pontoppidan was nevertheless not simply writing an autobiographical sketch: the narrator in the story is about forty-six years of age, and Pontoppidan himself was only thirty-six when his story was published. The span of time on which the effect of the story nominally depends was thus also a poetic invention. Once in Randers, the narrator is reminded of one Eleonora Ankersen, who had quite had his heart when he was thirteen or fourteen years of age and she eighteen. He determines to find out the details of her fate, which we know only to have been tragic. Little by little we learn of a village belle who does not know her own mind, who is secretly in love with a worthless cousin, and who, without desiring it, becomes engaged to a pedantic schoolteacher, but who feels compromised by the advances of a pompous army officer—and meets her death by drowning.

More than in any other tale, however, Pontoppidan here employs the device of retardation. After communicating to the reader a bit of titillating information and arousing some curiosity about Eleonora's fate, he regularly launches into a tangential anecdote or disconnected topographical observation, or he creates a confusion of reality and daydreams, so that a patina blurs the events pertaining to Eleonora. The real world is the traveller's Randers, with its capacity to evoke memories, in part through some of the persons the narrator meets again after thirty years' absence. The motivation for the tragedy is unconvincing, so that the book, unlike so many of Pontoppidan's other works, is without real ethical substance. Yet it does demonstrate that Pontoppidan could tell an entertaining story of a popular nature that could be borne up simply by his perspicacity as an observer and his skill in evolving images and associations for the reader.

In contrast, *Nattevagt* (*Night Watch*, 1894), has some parallels with the earlier stories in that it depicts a clash in life philosophies, although the ethical substance of the narrative is no longer one simply of social injustice or political repression. The genesis of *Nattevagt*—the title inevitably echoing Rembrandt— is temporally if not temperamentally associated with the genesis of *Det forjættede Land*. Pontoppidan wrote it subsequent to his sojourn in Italy in 1893, after having completed the second volume of his trilogy. The story is symbolic of the struggle between different directions in painting and literature in Denmark in the 1890s, but it is also a forthright depiction of the difficulties in adjustment between man and woman. The principal character, Jørgen Hallager, is a painter who is a champion of what might be called socialist realism. Just as Pontoppidan in some of his early stories was concerned with the oppression of the poor and underprivileged, so too Hallager paints scenes from everyday proletarian life. Hallager is very much an ambivalent figure. While he is a champion of justice for the poor in the abstract, he is inconsiderate and rude in his treatment of anyone who does not wholly accept his ideas. Like so many other Scandinavian artists of the nineteenth century, he has gone to Rome, but unlike them he is neither a neoclassicist nor an admirer of the ruins of classical antiquity which are found in the Eternal City. Before leaving Denmark, he became engaged to Ursula Brandt, the daughter of a wealthy man. Although she is very much in love with Hallager and they marry after her arrival in Rome, the two are wholly unsuited for each other. Hallager does not appreciate his wife's devotion and sensitivity, and fails to comprehend the affection which she retains for her father. Her efforts to reconcile her husband and her father are unsuccessful, but she makes every sacrifice in a futile attempt to please Hallager. Hallager, who possesses neither tact nor charity, is soon at odds with the entire Scandinavian colony in Rome and is full of indignation about what

Memoir and Pathos 79

he hears of his former friends and colleagues in Denmark who, he feels, have compromised themselves with the established order or who as poets and painters have given up their extreme naturalism and adopted new, idealistic styles. He is perhaps to be admired for his unwillingness to compromise his principles, but he in many ways is more bluster than productive. Ursula dies in Rome and Hallager returns to a changed Copenhagen where he finds himself nearly isolated. He marries a common woman with whom he had had an affair prior to the trip to Italy. At the end of the story Hallager expounds his theories to her, and is met with yawns. His hope is pinned on their tiny son, whom Hallager looks upon as a "recruit" in the lopsided struggle for truth and reality as he sees it.

To no small extent, Jørgen Hallager is an analogue to the figure of the little man in "Ilum Galgebakke." Both are uncompromising and inflexible in their demand for a proletarian revolution and for a realism that harbors neither dreams nor hazy idealism. The language that Hallager uses frequently suggests that of his counterpart in "Ilum Galgebakke." In fact, Hallager's last words are in the same spirit as those of the gnomic character from the earlier short story: "Keep the gall flowing!"

Also published in 1894 was the short novel *Den gamle Adam* (*The Old Adam*), which has the double function of exposing the suspension of good judgment in the face of superficial erotic attraction and, on a different level, of carrying on a discussion in the spirit of the preeminent critic and modernist, Georg Brandes. Brandes is represented by a "Dr. Levin" who in the story is reputed to have said that, for the greatest intellectual productivity, there is required "the most uninhibited freedom within the realm of Eros."[1] The allegorical Adam's weaknesses are observed to occur in everyman, and in the case of the novel in the person of the central character, Assessor Tofte. Peacefully and happily married and the head of a family, he is swept off his feet by a girl whom he meets at a summer resort. The somewhat surprising and quiet solution is his suit for divorce in order to follow the dictates of passion. From other stories by Pontoppidan, we know that the author is not sympathetic to this "Adam's" infatuation. Pontoppidan does not deny the existence and strength of passion, but he does not concur that it should destroy the fabric of the family and therewith society as he knew it. In a satirical intercalation in the novel, he lets a character say,

What would you like? Oh, divorce! Sørensen, a couple of chairs for the lady and gentleman; we shall be at your service right away; it will only take a moment and by paying a few crowns for a document, the state will with a twist of the wrist arrange for a home to be cast to the four winds, to make a couple of children fatherless and motherless, sign away their most sacred rights, and put the royal seal of shame and dishonor on the entire family. Such is the justice of our humanistic era.[2]

It is apparent that Pontoppidan's concern is not one of petty morality, of free love versus continence and chastity, but rather with the effects of a broken home on the innocent victims of divorce: the children. The argument that children may suffer more from a disharmonious marriage is not considered, but that is not the question. Rather, he is sounding a warning against the selfishness of men and women who are ready to dissolve their marriages for egocentric reasons without fully weighing the possible consequences.

In the next short novel, *Højsang* (*Hymn*, 1896), Pontoppidan seems scarcely true to himself. It is, in fact, a pastiche of the so-called "schoolteacher literature" which contains a dash of the widely read poet of the heath, Steen Steensen Blicher, plus a dash of regionalism; it is meant primarily to be entertaining while at the same time it is moralizing. Characters and situations are less than wholly credible, although the subtitle of this book (like that of *Den gamle Adam*) is a "sketch from everyday life." The melodramatic quality of the novel is evident. In fact, *Højsang* is the one novel by Pontoppidan which he rewrote in dramatic form, entitled *De vilde Fugle* (*The Wild Birds*, 1902). This suggests that Pontoppidan himself imputed to the story about an assistant from the Royal Library who seeks a rural idyll and discovers but another kind of chaos, an aesthetic and ethical substance which critics have been unwilling to accord to it. In the play, the story is simplified but made

Memoir and Pathos

more pointed. The suicide of the blustering, eccentric Lt. von Hacke is transformed on the stage into a virtually unmotivated and quick death. The conjugal problems of a country gentleman and his wife command the center of attention. The nominal narrator of the novel plays but a small role, although he is actually the *provocateur*.

The *raison d'être* for the book's subtitle is discovered only when one reads the novel. In the play there is no emphasis on pictures from country life; the secondary characters are either eliminated or become wholly background figures. The play is no picture of life seen, as it were, by him who lives by the side of the road. The characters of the play are too eccentric, too nearly grotesque, for the reader to be moved to identify with them. The tension between the landowner and his wife is removed from the great debate on sexual morality and women's rights and cannot furnish a basis for philosophical reflection. The fact that Pontoppidan created a dramatic situation in prose narrative was no assurance of effective drama. This particular effort is, rather, a demonstration that Pontoppidan was not successful as a dramatist.

It might be more accurate to say that Pontoppidan was not original as a dramatist, for his next play, *Asgaardsrejen* (*The Wild Huntsman*), contains so many echoes of Ibsen's dramas, that the reader—the play was produced on the stage only one season (1902–03)—has a sense of *déjà vu*. One concludes that, as a dramatist, Pontoppidan is out of his medium, although he was tempted to exploit the popularity of the naturalistic stage of the turn of the century.

If one looks beyond their differences to identify some characteristics common to the short novels of the 1890s, one cannot avoid mentioning the recurrent conflict between emotion and practicality, the tension engendered by erotic desire vis-à-vis bourgeois ambitions and the difficulty of establishing an acceptable and stable life pattern. Pontoppidan suggests the devils that, despite all rationalism and *bon sens*, plague the well-educated, productive individual. Intelligence, education, responsibility, affection, and good intentions are not enough to suppress the desire to gain greater spiritual satisfaction—but solely through temporal means.

We cannot consider Pontoppidan approaching the apex of his career as a narrator without mentioning the pathetic, concise, and transparent parable "Ørneflugt" ("Eagle's Flight," 1894) which has frequently been reprinted. It has sometimes been looked upon as a condensation of Pontoppidan's ethical message in the spirit of Darwinian naturalism: you cannot expect to live the life of an eagle if you have grown up in a farmyard surrounded by domestic fowl. The brief didactic tale is found in the second edition (1899) of a collection of—for Pontoppidan atypical—parables entitled *Krøniker* (*Chronicles*, 1890).

The short tale has associations with various themes that inform many of Pontoppidan's works. A tame eagle, dubbed with the unaquiline name "Klaus," has grown up in a barnyard, and a clergyman's barnyard at that. He breaks away from his pedestrian surroundings only when, as a sexually mature bird, he is attracted to a passing she-eagle. With difficulty arising from want of practice and exercise, he follows her far, only to give up the chase exhausted and to seek to return to the security of the barnyard. Approaching it, Klaus is mistaken for a bird of prey that would attack the chickens and is shot down. The moral is inescapable. We are reminded of a series of pitiful figures Pontoppidan created whose spirits have known only oppression and who have lacked either the opportunity or the courage to be themselves, to test their mettle, and to liberate themselves from exploitation.

It is an oversimplification to see in this single parable the epitome of Pontoppidan's work. To be sure, the parable suggests much that is essential in the early tales, but it misses an abundance of other characteristics that assure Pontoppidan his place in literary history: the search for a life philosophy, the incisive depiction of the times, the psychological insight, and the crystal clarity of presentation. "Ørneflugt" does remain a minor classic of modern Danish literature, however, and may even be used as an introduction to Pontoppidan if the reader is informed that there is more to Pontoppidan than didactic naturalism.

CHAPTER 9

Will and Testament

I Life Refracted

Lykke-Per (*Lucky Per*) is a psychological novel of development. It is also partially autobiographical, notably in its first volume, subtitled "Hans Ungdom" ("His Youth," 1898). In addition, it is an incisively analytical description of Denmark in the 1890s. It is best known for this last characteristic. While the effect of the novel upon its readers is a result of Pontoppidan's naturalism, from the fact that the reader encounters situations and experiences analogous to his or her own, the renown of the novel derives from its historical and interpretive quality. The 1880s and 90s were times of particular and identifiable change in Denmark, away from the distinctively agrarian society into which Pontoppidan was born in 1854 toward the industrial and technologically oriented society it was to become in the twentieth century.

The imaginative writer can create a reality which engenders insight and understanding of change in a way that the pragmatic historian may not. The writer can concentrate many events and a multitude of conditions in a limited area or even in the person of one protagonist. He can place that protagonist in a series of loosely connected situations which, taken together, allow a comprehensive synthesis of complex events. He can imbue the protagonist with traits typifying a given time or society. The hero of Pontoppidan's novel, Per Sidenius, is, like so many of his contemporaries in the 1890s, an optimist. He believes that technology and industry will create a better world and that the future of civilization lies in the hands of the technocrat, the engineer, the industrialist, the financier. Like Pontoppidan himself, Per Sidenius comes to Copenhagen in order to study engineering at the Polytechnical Institute. He gives up his course of study for different reasons than Pontoppidan did. Pontoppidan had been moved to write about certain conditions that he saw, and he was able to formulate effectively in words what he deplored in society. His hero, however, full of overconfidence and driven by ambition, is impatient with the requirements that he learn the basics of mathematics and engineering which would possibly enable him to execute the vast plans that he works out on paper and dreams about. Pontoppidan does not intend primarily to describe the society of the time, but he does provide an abundance of information about the older society and the newer society, about the "provinces" and the capital, so that the reader acquires an understanding of the time from the novel.

Per comes from the most conservative of backgrounds; his father is a clergyman who has little appreciation for childish merriment or the need for entertainment and no understanding of the dreams which motivate his son. He, and the rest of Per's family, are devoted to the status quo while Per dreams only of change. When Per comes to Copenhagen, he soon exchanges his homespun ways for the materialism of the capital. He gains new friends, some of dubious reputation, and acquires a different standard of values. In the tradition of the novel of development, ultimately following Goethe's *Wilhelm Meister*, Pontoppidan's Per Sidenius experiences many levels of society, but despite the promise in his name, "Lucky-Per," (a name familiar to all Danes since it is the title of one of Andersen's tales), he is really a failure at everything he undertakes. Not until the final and eighth volume of the novel does he ultimately find himself while leading the hermit's life on the west coast of Jutland.

The novel begins with a detailed description not of Peter Andreas Sidenius (Lykke-Per) but of his father and of the dour and puritanical mood that pervades the manse in the small Jutland city (identical with Randers, where Pontoppidan grew up under similar circumstances) in which Per spent his childhood. We learn of the tension between Pastor Sidenius and his fellow citizens, who are of a worldly cast, and of the difference in attitude towards the state religion between its sincere advocate and practitioner on the one hand, and self-satisfied burghers on the other. For them, Lutheran Christianity is expected to

Will and Testament

be a comforting adjunct to daily life rather than a stern reminder of the Ten Commandments or the Sermon on the Mount.

Such a lengthy beginning unrelated to the experiences of the protagonist may seem to the inexperienced reader of Pontoppidan somewhat misleading and disembodied from the nucleus of the narrative. He who comes to *Lykke-Per* from earlier works by Pontoppidan, however, realizes that the stage is being set for the development of the narrative and for the crystalization of the ethos that will inform the entire work. Pontoppidan is insinuating into his reader's subconscious the importance of Per's background and his early religious training, although that may seem to have gone unheeded by young Per. Pontoppidan is also suggesting that this background is going to play a greater role for Per than might otherwise be presaged by the first few volumes of the series.

In Copenhagen, Per Sidenius makes several acquaintances who change the course of his life radically. One of these is a civil servant named Neergaard and another is Mrs. Engelhardt, with whom Per has his first love affair after Neergaard commits suicide and rather surprisingly wills money to Per. Per's infatuation for Mrs. Engelhardt is very brief and comes to a sudden close when he comes to the realization that Neergaard and she had an intimate relationship earlier. Once more the contrast between Per's background and his life in Copenhagen is stressed. At this juncture, Per finds out that his father's days are numbered, as he is suffering from cancer. Per is beset by his conscience for not yet having made something of himself while his father still is alive—that is, not having rehabilitated himself in his father's eyes.

II *The Dream*

In the second of the eight small volumes that constitute the first edition of *Lykke-Per*, *Lykke-Per finder Skatten* (*Lykke-Per Finds the Treasure*, 1898), Per Sidenius aggressively attempts to make a place for himself in society and succeeds in compromising himself on several fronts. Driven by ambition and erotic impulses, Per sacrifices his own ideals for the vague image of material success. His ambition is to be a successful engineer by establishing a new free port and a system of canals in Jutland and by tapping new sources of waterpower, and to do this in the vicinity of his native town in order to rehabilitate himself in the eyes of the family—to "show them." He does not heed the admonitions of his teachers at the Polytechnical Institute in Copenhagen and abandons his formal studies in order to execute a grandiose plan on paper. While the failure to achieve immediate success discourages him temporarily, he casts about for a new source of support. It fortuitously appears on the horizon in the form of a wealthy Jewish family, the Salomons, with two unmarried daughters.

Per already has some fleeting erotic adventures behind him. For a time he has enjoyed an innocent relationship with the niece of a neighbor in the complex of dwellings for retired seamen where he lives. She is a girl from the provinces, the daughter of a saddler, who is spending some time in the capital. The two young people are first casually attracted to one another and then gradually become good friends and exchange a few kisses. Had Per been guided only by his naive and erotic inclination rather than his ambition, he might have spent a happy life with his Franciska. When he is surprised by the girl's uncle and must answer point blank whether his intentions are honorable and whether or not he wants to marry the girl, he makes a quick and negative decision. Franciska's devotion is outweighed by Per's dream of future fame and success. He has now sacrificed something pure and intrinsically valuable, but he feels no remorse for having played with the serious emotions of an inexperienced girl.

There are numerous analogues in literature to which one might point. The nearest at hand within the context of Danish literature is the relationship between the figures of Adam Homo and Alma in the nineteenth-century epic poem *Adam Homo* (1841–48), by the Danish poet Frederick Paludan-Müller (1809–76) which has been viewed as a Danish analogue to Goethe's *Faust*. While it is safe to assume that Pontoppidan had read *Adam Homo*, he was not using Paludan-Müller as a model. The situation is simply too common and all too human to need explanation by means of a search for models and influences.

Per does not realize it, but he has in fact suffered a defeat.

Will and Testament

Another defeat of a different nature soon overcomes him: the head of the society of engineers in the Danish capital agrees to examine the plans of Per's extravagant project of canals and a free port. For a short time Per lives in a fool's paradise, for he cannot envisage that the plans could be brusquely pushed aside as fanciful, but such turns out to be the case. Per nevertheless remains convinced of the brilliance and viability of his plans. Not for the last time, an identification with Caesar (made by Ivan Salomon) echoes in his mind. Per still believes himself a child of fortune; he willingly accepts Caesar's words as his motto: "I came, I saw, I conquered."

Per now pins his hopes to the House of Salomon as a source of financial support which would permit him to realize his plans to revolutionize Danish transportation and ultimately the Danish economy. He is first attracted to the younger daughter Nanny and repulsed by her somewhat older half-sister Jakobè. With various other ambitious men, Per cultivates the Salomon family; he is in actuality a protégé of Jakobè's brother Ivan, who is convinced of Per's genius. The physical attractions of Nanny gradually wane before the intellectual superiority of Jakobè, and at the end of volume two, Per surprises himself by asking whether it is indeed Jakobè rather than Nanny with whom he is in love. Per's willingness to compromise for ambition is reflected by his interest in the Salomons. While he is erotically attracted to the one sister and then finds he is in love with the other, both attraction and love are tempered by the glimmer of gold. In point of fact, the Salomon fortune is the real attraction of both half-sisters. In order to obtain respect and credence, and in order to find practical acceptance of his grandiose plans, Per believes that he must have command of a large amount of money. Not without some misgiving does he entertain the thought of taking a Jewish wife. While he had not known any Jews before he came to Copenhagen, his conservative Christian upbringing has instilled its modicum of anti-Semitism in him, which Jakobè senses. Jakobè is keenly aware of her heritage and has had to suffer for it, in part because, unlike her half-sister, she is exotic and un-Danish in appearance. The petty persecution and prejudice that she felt as a child have made her unwilling to take any husband; she does not want to bring a child into the world who will undergo experiences comparable to her own. For this reason she will not even marry a Jew, while the thought of marrying a Gentile is totally unacceptable.

Pontoppidan reinforces Jakobè's reactions to the petty anti-Semitism in nineteenth-century Denmark by describing her experience in a Berlin railway station: here she had seen hundreds of Jews in utmost need as they were being transported from Russia through Germany to the New World as a result of the Russian pogroms against the Jews. The sight made her rebellious at the same time that it sickened her. Pontoppidan, with whose critical stance toward the established church we are now familiar, subtly lets Jakobè inveigh against those pulpits from which the gospel of love is proclaimed at the same time that human beings are being treated without compassion a few streets away.

The second volume differs stylistically not only from the first but also from Pontoppidan's previous works in that there is considerably less description of landscape or surroundings. While this is explicable merely because the second volume is a continuation of the first and does not begin an entirely new narrative, the emphasis on Per's inward reflections and outward experiences is notable. There is here a different kind of narrative from that in the first volume. One can, in fact, almost speak of a series of novellas making up the second volume. Most clear-cut is the love story of Per and Franciska which constitutes chapter two.

III *False Promise*

Per does win the heart of Jakobè in the third volume, *Lykke-Per, Hans Kærlighed* (*Lykke-Per, His Love,* 1899), and he is convinced that he is as lucky as his nickname would indicate. It has not been easy for him to overcome resistance on the part of Jakobè and her family and only after considerable give and take and questionable deportment has he achieved his immediate goal. There is nevertheless a dark undercurrent sensed at the end of volume three in a conversation between Jakobè and Per's brother Eberhard Sidenius, and shortly thereafter a second message that Per's father's days are numbered

Will and Testament

arrives. This does not deter Per from carrying out his plan to travel through Europe in order to acquaint himself with engineers and engineering projects which may have some bearing upon his utopian plan to establish a system of canals in Denmark as an alternative to expanding the railway system, and to exploit waves and tides as a source of hydroelectric power. Cool heads have judged Per to be a dreamer and his plans to be impractical. He nevertheless has been able to arouse some interest for his project, and with money furnished by the Salomons he is publishing a book in which the project is explained.

Much of the narrative in the third volume is not concerned directly with Per but rather with the Salomon family and the many connections that it has with Danish society at the time and with events of the day. Some contemporary figures are introduced and others are alluded to. The most important of these in the background is "Dr Nathan" (in reality, Georg Brandes), champion of new ideas from the outside world, who serves Per Sidenius as a source of inspiration.

The reader recognizes the great contrast that exists between Per's dour Christian background and the enlightened Jewish community represented by the Salomons. While Pontoppidan tends to be critical of the background that he shared with Per Sidenius, he is not without sympathy for the earnestness and sincerity of the Christian and nationally oriented life which Per rejects, as well as the non-Christian, supranational stance represented by Philip Salomon and his household. The contrast between these two attitudes towards life is too great for one to expect them easily to be reconciled. As a consequence, the reader is left with an uneasy feeling that the union of Per and Jakobè Salomon will be a mesalliance quite as much as was that of the city-born and sophisticated Emanuel Hansted and the simple country girl he married.

This third volume of *Lykke-Per* is pre-eminently a psychological depiction of Per Sidenius. There is little description and almost no attention is paid to natural surroundings. Per's development—or change in attitudes, if one will—is central to the narrative. His attitudes and reactions toward the various persons with whom he associates are of primary importance, but all his experiences now have some relation to the Salomon family. He is drawn into a different world than the one from which he has sprung—a world which he cannot fully accept, although he repeatedly rejects his own origins. Unwittingly, he is moving into a spiritual no man's land, while at the same time he arrogantly and stubbornly retains faith in himself. Objectively viewed, he would be said to have experienced only defeat, but he doggedly refuses to acknowledge either defeat or the well-grounded reasons for nonacceptance by persons who are skeptical of his great plans. His confidence evokes admiration both from Jakobè Salomon and her brother Ivan, however. Ivan manages to have their uncle Heinrich arrange for Per to be given a loan which will enable him to travel and visit various Central-European engineering undertakings which should have bearing on Per's own projects. The reader's sympathies can only be with Jakobè, who gives evidence of being an upright and self-sacrificing person. Her visit (to be sure, without Per's knowledge) to Per's brother Eberhard is in reality an indictment of the narrow-mindedness of smug Lutheran Christianity. Time and again she is the butt of senseless anti-Semitic remarks and now she must suffer the indignity of Eberhard's chastising her for failing to recognize the "truth" of Christianity, *nota bene* his own brand of Christianity. At this relatively early stage in the narrative, Jakobè emerges as the incipient heroine of the story, another Gretchen to Per's Faust. She, too, is to be sacrificed upon the altar of Per's ambition.

IV *Nadir*

Per's struggle with his heritage dominates the fourth volume, *Lykke-Per i det Fremmede* (*Lykke-Per Abroad*, 1899). After his first glowing days in Berlin, Per had received a telegram, in answer to his own inquiry, that his father was dying. He made a sudden decision to return home for a day, but the day stretched into a fortnight. Not only had his father's death in itself made an impression upon him, but the reaction of the townsmen to the death of their old clergyman astonished him. In his childhood he had been ashamed of his father and his father's position in society. He is now astounded to discover that his father's death brings forth a great outpouring of emotion from the wealthy as well as the poor and from members

Will and Testament

of the government and the military in his native city. He is surprised to find that the entire community respected his father and mourned his demise. Far from being a ridiculous servant of a moribund church, the father turned out to have been the corporate conscience of the community, the sort of uncompromising moralist whom most people secretly admire. As the uniformed representatives of church and state appear for Per's father's funeral, one of his proudest dreams is fulfilled in an unexpected way, "a dream from the time he envisaged himself as a changeling, a kidnapped prince, who in the end would find his way back to his father's mansions."[1] For a moment after his father's funeral, Per gives vent to his true feelings in a letter written to Jakobè. No sooner has he written the letter than he tears it up and substitutes a matter-of-fact communication which, to be sure, does not entirely obscure the truth from his intuitive fiancée.

Returning to Berlin, he continues with considerably less conviction than before to carry out his plans. The sincerity of his attachment to Jakobè Salomon is seriously questioned twice, first by the temptation to consider the possibility of winning the hand of the heiress to a still greater fortune and second by the sensuous attractiveness of a country girl from southern Germany. Much of the narrative is devoted to letters written by Per to Jakobè, and in the letters the reader, and Jakobè, sense a change in Per's attitudes.

While we observe Per at his honor's nadir in volume four, we also recognize more clearly than before his basic problem. On the one hand, he cannot escape from the religious scruples with which his upbringing has inculcated him. On the other, he cannot find or create a life philosophy that would give him peace of mind. Outwardly he is the champion of a new technology and enjoys access to creative efforts of constructive modern engineering related in practice and theory to the project that he has proposed in his book—that was coolly received after his departure from Denmark. Inwardly he is a god-seeker. Once established in an Alpine village near a dam and flood control project, he becomes more and more deeply involved in religious and philosophical speculation, clearly accentuated or induced by his father's death. Without realizing the implication of the decision, he determines not to leave the village until he has achieved some sort of personal philosophy. He becomes less and less satisfied with himself and becomes spiritually farther removed from his fiancée. He begins to question his own values and becomes a victim of the very tradition of religious introspection he is endeavoring to escape. At this juncture Jakobè appears suddenly and unexpectedly, and Per is brought back to a sort of reality. He now feels that he really loves Jakobè and finds solace in her arms. The fourth volume ends on a grotesque note, with Per producing a revolver and shooting at a wayside crucifix in an endeavor once more to divorce himself from his own background.

From the standpoint of form, the fourth volume is at once set off from the previous three by the use of the epistolary technique: the narrative is continued through a series of letters written by Per to Jakobè. There is no longer an endeavor to create the sort of narrative autonomy that the previous three volumes possessed. If one were not familiar with the story prior to the opening of volume four, it would not be comprehensible. Pontoppidan did provide a sort of crutch or compromise from the second volume of the series onward by giving a résumé of the story on the verso of the title page, but the six-sentence résumé at the beginning of volume four is no satisfactory substitute for familiarity with the earlier parts of the novel.

In the first chapter, the epistolary form is only used for the first twenty pages, whereupon the attention of the reader is turned to Copenhagen and the family Salomon, but in the third chapter, the device of the letter is reintroduced and dominates the chapter. As in many epistolary novels, the letter serves at least three practical functions. It provides the reader an apparent access to the workings of a character's mind that would be difficult to achieve merely through descriptive narration. It permits jumps in time and action that might otherwise seem to be arbitrary and ill-founded. Insofar as there are other sources of factual information accessible to the reader besides the letters, it also gives him an opportunity to ascertain the adequacy or inadequacy of a character in communicating the truth.

Will and Testament

This third epistolary function is pronounced in volume four of *Lykke-Per*, for Per reveals himself as something of a scoundrel. He is attracted to Jakobè's Berlin cousin for the simple reason that the cousin is heiress to a much greater fortune than is Jakobè. Momentarily, he has the incredible cheek to imagine that Jakobè would understand, should she be abandoned for her cousin, since such a switch would give Per greater assurance of worldly success. On Per's part, this contemptuous line of thought is but a pipedream, however, and soon dissolves, to be superseded by other extravagant ideas.

V *Counterforces*

The fifth volume of *Lykke-Per* (1901) carries the ironic subtitle, *Hans store Værk* (*His Great Work*). In the entire volume Per Sidenius accomplishes nothing. While he is in Rome experiencing highly ambivalent feelings toward his fiancée Jakobè, Jakobè's brother Ivan Salomon, his champion in Copenhagen, is trying every means to interest a consortium to finance the project that Per has proposed in his recently published book. Per no longer has any active interest in his own proposal, but nevertheless continues to have visions of grandeur. While a bust of him is being made at the behest of the sister of his late benefactor, de Neergaard, Per believes he has discovered a visible similarity between himself and a bust of Caesar and encourages the sculptor to see a likeness.

In sending Per to Rome, Pontoppidan was following good European tradition established in the eighteenth century: the young man who was learning to know the world or who was on the Grand Tour did indeed go to Rome. Italy was long an essential part of the *Lehr-und Wanderjahre* of the Western European. The association with Rome is for Per a bit more subtle, however. He has felt himself to be a Caesar, and experiencing Caesar's Rome only accentuates his vision of grandeur. He has once before felt that he had "come, seen, and conquered." He feels that the direction of his future is set, the die is cast, and he actually uses Caesar's proverbial Latin phrase, *jacta alea est*. The extent of his delusion is emphasized by his desire to see a similarity between Caesar's features and his own.

Whereas in the fourth volume the reader was privy only to Per's letters to Jakobè, Pontoppidan uses Jakobè's letters to Per as a major device in the fifth volume. The letters serve to preserve a bond between the two worlds of Copenhagen and Rome, between the efforts to realize Per's dreams through channels of the Danish business community and Per's supercilious life in the Eternal City. In Rome he is divorced from the reality in which Jacobè and Ivan Salomon, his two most ardent admirers, exist. Jakobè's lengthy and emotional missives are in touching contrast to Per's growing aversion to letter writing and the curtness of his replies. When the newly married Nanny Salomon and her husband visit Rome, Per is once more attracted to her and determines temporarily to break off the relationship with Jakobè, unaware of the fact that Jakobè is pregnant.

When Per returns to Copenhagen he meets the financiers Ivan has interested in his project. The meeting turns out to be disastrous, for Per will accept no compromise. He assumes the position that he is doing Danish capitalists a favor, instead of attempting to curry their favor by seeking a reconciliation with Colonel Bjerregaard, head of the society of Danish engineers, known to us from volume two. He is received coolly at his prospective parents-in-law that evening, but Philip Salomon refrains from expressing an opinion about the judgment Per has shown. The plans for a formal dinner to announce Per and Jakobè's engagement the next evening are not abandoned. Returning to Copenhagen from the Salomon estate that night, Per is drawn to the address where his mother and sisters now live on a small side street. He stands in the darkness staring up at a dimly lighted window in which he sees an object that reminds him of his childhood.

A certain inconsistency in the portrayal of Jakobè had been evident in volume four: she was no longer particularly homely, unhealthy, or Semitic in appearance as had been the case in Pontoppidan's first descriptions of her. Indeed, she seems to be rather a different woman: attractive, almost pretty in appearance, smartly dressed, radiant and glowing, with no stress on her Semitic heritage. In volume five, however, she reverts to the Jakobè of the early part of the narrative. While Pontoppidan may be faulted for furnishing descriptions of the same person that, when abstracted from the story, would seem to be inconsistent, one should remember that much of the time the reader is seeing Jakobè through Per's eyes. As he is alternately more and less attracted to Jakobè erotically, those features that would be less attractive to him are glossed over, or, as the case may be, emphasized. No other character undergoes as much outward change as Jakobè (disregarding the matter of mere clothing, for Per's changes in dressing habits are striking).

VI *Crisis*

The sixth volume of the novel is entitled *Lykke-Per og hans Kæreste* (*Lykke-Per and his Fiancée*, 1902), and is clearly an extension of the fifth, with much description of life in the Salomon household and Per's ambivalent relationship to the several members of the Salomon family. The entire volume spans only a few days' time, but they are critical, for they include the announcement of Per's engagement to Jakobè, an altered relationship between the engaged couple, and the death of Per's mother. The announcement of the engagement is an elaborate social event with some hundred guests. It was conceived as interlocking with the establishment of a company to execute Per's plans. With that possibility cashiered, the occasion is less than successful, and is compounded by a sudden erotically tinged confrontation between Jakobè's half-sister Nanny and Per. After the engagement dinner itself, Per wanders off alone, only to observe Danish families in their gardens acting much like his own family and very unlike the urbane Salomons and their wealthy or intellectual guests.

Much of the time Per seems to be in such an evil humor that Jakobè is afraid to inform him of her condition and instead encourages him in his desire to visit America. At this junction he accidentally learns that his mother has died. Despite his efforts to seem indifferent to the news, he is inwardly deeply moved. When informed by a brother that the corpse of their mother is to be transported by ship from Copenhagen to Jutland that evening, he goes to the harbor to watch the coffin be loaded on the ship. He suddenly makes a decision to accompany the casket on its voyage, unbeknownst to his family and friends. This happens at the very juncture when there is renewed interest in his plans for a free port and power plant and when previous adversaries seek to smooth out their differences with him. Without his knowing it, Per's decision to follow his mother's corpse to Jutland bursts the bubble of his dream world. He leaves the possibility of power and wealth behind him in Copenhagen as he is overtaken by memories of the past and pricked by his Protestant bourgeois conscience.

In the large part of the narrative devoted to social activity at the Salomons, almost a third of the entire sixth volume, there is a curious intercalation which pertains only tangentially to Per: a description of "Dr. Nathan" and his position in contemporary Danish intellectual life. While the assessment and criticism of Dr. Nathan, clearly a representation of Georg Brandes, might seem somewhat out of place if judged merely from the standpoint of the development of Per and Jakobè, he is an unavoidable figure if the reader is to obtain a "picture of the times" from *Lykke-Per*. Brandes was a central figure in Danish intellectual life from the 1870s until after World War I. Moreover, some of Brandes's basic assumptions were also the basic assumptions of Per Sidenius, viz. that Denmark was a backward country that had to catch up with the modernity of the great industrialized nations of the West. Brandes was looking for a literary renewal and championed naturalistic literature that dealt with current problems. Per Sidenius felt the impact of the Brandesian affirmation in that it helped generate a faith in technology and in the ability of technology to solve the economic and social problems inherited from the past.

VII *Apostasy*

In the first edition of *Lykke-Per* the eight volumes bear individual titles. The title of the second volume (*Lykke-Per finds the Treasure*) is meant ironically, for although Per does acquire material fortune temporarily, he does not find a treasure worth the name. The most ironic title, however, is that of volume seven, *Lykke-Per. Hans Rejse til Amerika* (*Lykke-Per. His Journey to America*, 1903), for the journey to America is only a projection that never materializes. Per does not again leave Denmark.

Will and Testament

The surroundings, people, and daily life which Per Sidenius experiences in the seventh volume provide an absolute contrast to the previous volume, which had been dominated by descriptions of the Salomon family and Per's relation to them. Once in Jutland—with the ulterior motive of obtaining a new loan—Per determines to visit the wealthy woman whom he met in Rome. He is hospitably received on the Prangen estate, "Kjærsholm,"[2] and enjoys the relief of country life away from the pressures of Copenhagen and away from Jakobè. Per is now able to appreciate his natural surroundings and to see in the undulating Danish landscape a veritable Eden. He is attracted to an outgoing Grundtvigian clergyman and his daughter Inger, who at first reminds him strongly of his erstwhile innocent love, Franciska, the saddler's daughter. This identification is but one of many which suggest the cyclical quality of the narrative—or, perhaps more precisely, the cyclical development of Per's life in the narrative. Days turn into weeks at the estate as Per becomes more and more spiritually removed from Jakobè and drawn back into his Lutheran heritage.

Here and there in the story flashbacks to Per's childhood and upbringing deter or even limit him in using his imagination. Even his early religious training helps build a barrier between him and Jakobè Salomon. There is a turning point in Per's spiritual life when he suddenly decides to attend church services one Sunday morning, but only after the people on the estate have left for the church of Pastor Blomberg. By chance he reaches not Blomberg's church but the poorly attended church of a nearby clergyman, one Pastor Fjaltring, who is identified by the followers of Blomberg as a heretical madman. Per, puzzled by Fjaltring's emotionalism in the pulpit, mentally dismisses him, only to meet up with him the next day.

While Jakobè has been serious and self-sacrificing in her devotion to Per, Per has been superficial and self-seeking in his relationship to her. Jakobè is in reality the heroine of the book, loving, sincere, and altruistic. She has the virtues which Per lacks. Because of their basic differences and misunderstandings, the engagement is broken, and Per does not learn that Jakobè bears him a child. He remains the dreamer who attempts to build on sand. He is unwilling to accept the fact that there is something fantastic about his projects; he is unwilling to accept criticism. The "great work" of which he dreams and which provides the subtitle for the fifth volume in the series never comes to fruition.

At the very juncture when Per is ready to depart from Jutland to undertake the oft-mentioned and important journey to America, he realizes that the attraction to Pastor Blomberg's daughter Inger is mutual. "It was like having a glimpse into the bright magnificence of Paradise while passing through the gloomy abyss of the kingdom of darkness."[3] He is overcome by his conscience and feels that he is deserving of punishment because he has sold his soul to Mammon. Removed only by a short distance and a few minutes from the social gathering at Kjærsholm at which he had announced his impending departure and had taken leave of Inger, he sinks down on his knees and sobs out to God that he deserves his punishment and admits his sins. That night his Christianity awakens within him. In his mind's eye he breaks with his past and gives himself up to his forefathers' God. A necessary corollary is his formally breaking his engagement with Jakobè; and the journey to America has to be abandoned. After subsequently taking leave of Pastor Blomberg he is caught in the rain and seeks shelter in a barn where, by chance, Pastor Fjaltring is also waiting out the storm. A short exchange of ideas with the unhappy clergyman leaves Per a bit puzzled, but he is unable entirely to forget the image of Pastor Fjaltring.

One can say that Per has returned to the fold. His ambitions become very modest. Realizing that he must find some way of making a living, he decides to study to become a surveyor. To do this he must return to Copenhagen for a time to prepare himself and take the surveyor's examination. After having visited his childhood home in Jutland, Per arrives in Copenhagen the same day that Jakobè arrives in Berlin on her way to Silesia, where she will secretly give birth to Per's child, who is fated to die in infancy.

VIII *Cognition*

At the beginning of the eighth and final volume of *Lykke-Per*, *Hans sidste Kamp* (*His last Struggle*, 1904), Per Sidenius has

Will and Testament

returned to Copenhagen in order to finish his studies so that he may at least become a surveyor. The new sojourn in Copenhagen brings much humiliation with it, and Per, sick in body and spirit, must finally accept a loan from his brothers and sisters. After concluding his studies and taking his examination, he serves six months in the Danish army prior to returning to Jutland. Once there, he develops a new pattern of existence rapidly. He becomes engaged to the daughter of Pastor Blomberg, marries her, and establishes himself as a surveyor and engineer involved with local problems. Per is drawn more and more to Pastor Fjaltring, the antithesis of his father-in-law, because of Fjaltring's seriousness and sincerity, which subconsciously reminds Per of his own father.

Pontoppidan now moves the story along rapidly. Several years pass almost without comment; Per and his wife Inger have three children and are settled down into a comfortable rural routine. Per's struggle for a life philosophy is not over, however. The news that Pastor Fjaltring has committed suicide unnerves him, and the realization that his grandiose plans of earlier years are being exploited by another man without his receiving any credit injects a new element of dissatisfaction into his consciousness. Through Inger, Per is made aware of the moodiness and arbitrariness he displays in dealing with his own children, and he eventually becomes troubled by the thought that they may inherit the same curse that he feels lies upon him. He becomes more and more irritated with the superficiality of his father-in-law Pastor Blomberg, and this ultimately leads to an irreparable break between them. Per feels that the only solution which will benefit his children is for him to remove himself from his family, and he lets Inger believe that he has been unfaithful to her so that she will seek a separation. While Per has now transcended the traditional religious belief that he had embraced once again during his visit to Jutland, he cries out in anguish to the God in whom he no longer believes.

Per, relieved of all ambitions, now seeks and obtains a lowly position as a road inspector in northwestern Jutland. Here at last he is able to come to terms with himself, no longer tempted by the false gods of wealth and power. After Per's death from cancer, he is found to have left all his worldly goods to the school which Jakobè Salomon had established in Copenhagen. In preparing Per's possessions for auction, the local schoolteacher comes upon a kind of diary which Per kept in his last years, containing religious and philosophical observations about nature and God, life, and faith. The diary gives the reader insight into Per Sidenius's real psyche. What he should have known and understood early in life has come to him as a late realization. He has chased after a chimera rather than accepting reality and trying to live within its limitations to the best of his ability. The final words that the schoolteacher reads from Per's diary mention, "The true faith, truth in nature, rich, wise, merciful nature, which has a cure for everything, which generally replaces on the one hand what we have lost on the other...."[4]

IX Lykke-Per *as a Novel*

Since the advent of the novel of development (German: *Entwicklungsroman, Bildungsroman*) which in its modern form dates from the early eighteenth century, first with Henry Fielding's *Tom Jones*, and then in a renewed and influential model with Goethe's *Wilhelm Meister*, the hero's experiences acquaint him with various elements of society. Pontoppidan hews to this pattern in *Lykke-Per*. There is not only the contrast of a clerical versus a worldly home in his younger years, of small town life versus life in the Danish capital, but also the experiencing of the petit bourgeois, the bourgeois, and the aristocracy of money, and of the artistic circles. The intent is not only to provide the main character with disparate experiences but also to depict the society in which he lives, providing the reader with a comprehensive survey of the background before which the story plays.

For the contemporary Danish reader, Henrik Pontoppidan's *Lykke-Per* was also a *roman-à-clef*. Numerous persons who were described in the novel were fairly transparent to Pontoppidan's contemporaries, although the fact that Pontoppidan used living models for various of the characters in *Lykke-Per* is of no consequence to us today, with the possible exception of the figure of Doctor Nathan, who was supposed to be Georg

Brandes.⁵ Georg Brandes's lectures had called attention to the need for a foreign orientation in literature for Scandinavia. But hand in hand with the foreign orientation in literature went an orientation to the societies of other Western countries, notably England. England with its technology, industry, and shipping was the most admired model, but there was also considerable orientation to France and Germany. This new outlook is depicted in Pontoppidan's novel. Doctor Nathan appears as the intellectual leader of the times and the important Danish financiers, many of whom are Jewish, are seen in something of a European perspective. Even the acceptance and assimilation of Jews in Danish society is worked into the novel.

For today's reader many of the topical allusions may be unimportant or even not understood, although the novel still can be appreciated as a multi-faceted representation of Denmark at the end of the nineteenth century. Equally important, however, is the philosophical ethos of the novel. The ethical object lessons, somewhat exaggerated as they may be, confront the reader, who to a greater or lesser extent shares flaws of character with Pontoppidan's protagonist. The ultimate message in the novel is not new: to thy own self be true. In Pontoppidan's novel this message has no sense of banality or platitude.

The novel has had an impact on succeeding generations of readers and has been acclaimed as a masterpiece of world literature by such diverse voices as Thomas Mann and Georg Lukács.⁶ Translations into nine languages have been published, though not one in English.⁷ Every critic of Danish literature has at one time or other spoken his piece about the novel,⁸ and the amassed testimony is of an imaginative work which affects the thought and lives of its readers, a realistic presentation which has intrinsic historical validity, and situations and characters that are identifiable within the realm of the average reader's experience. One Danish critic, Jørgen Bukdahl (1896–) has called Per Sidenius a modern Don Quixote,⁹ but Per is only a Don Quixote insofar as Everyman also carries a Don Quixote within him. Per is an *alter ego* not only of his creator Pontoppidan but of the average human being insofar as he is part dreamer and fantast. The reader of the novel smarts under Per's mistakes, for they could easily be his own mistakes. The reader is often grateful to Pontoppidan for pointing out those errors in judgment which we all sometimes make, but which we may possibly avoid because we have made the acquaintance of Per Sidenius.

The overall and lasting impact of the novel is well attested by a collection of documents edited by Knut Ahnlund and published as *Omkring Lykke-Per* (*About Lykke-Per*) in 1971. Ahnlund assembled over 300 pages of criticism of the novel from the appearance of its first volume in 1898 until the year 1970. An appended bibliography lists scores of other sources which can be consulted for additional criticism and comment about the novel.

It cannot be considered surprising that the several small volumes that make up the first edition of *Lykke-Per* did not meet everywhere with unmitigated enthusiasm. Some critics,[10] whose judgments have borne up best in the course of time, were kindly disposed and receptive, although even they were uncertain of Pontoppidan's direction of thought in the first few volumes. Others were openly hostile and denigrating. The most influential and articulate of this latter group was the critic-clergyman Oscar Geismar (1877–1950) who, perhaps because of his own occupational bias, was offended by Per Sidenius's (and therefore presumably Henrik Pontoppidan's) attitude toward the Christian religion, an attitude that Geismar identified bluntly as a "hatred of Christianity."[11] Geismar recognized Pontoppidan's skill as a narrator and acknowledged his ability to create a gallery of convincing characters, but he felt these characters to be functioning in a world beyond good and evil—and the allusion was directly to Friedrich Nietzsche, as Geismar cited the phrase in German: "jenseits Gutes und Böses." For Geismar, Per Sidenius was a jellylike character without backbone, an individual who lacked idealism and presumably could therefore not serve any acceptable didactic purpose.

One wonders whether the Reverend Dean Geismar's criticism was not in part generated by the positive attitude toward Jews which Pontoppidan displays in the novel. After all, if *Lykke-Per* has a heroine she is Per's Jewish fiancée Jacobè Salomon, the members of whose family are on the whole depicted sympathetically. In some of the early criticism of Pontoppidan's novel there is identifiable a petty, rankling anti-Semitism, in part perhaps because Pontoppidan's representatives of the established Church make a rather sorry impression, having neither the character nor the charity, and perhaps not the faith and the hope of the stronger-willed Jewish figures. As the twentieth century wore on, Pontoppidan's acid allusions to the established Christian religion and his tolerance toward Judaism no longer caused offense; his countrymen came to a large extent to share his views. What is more, Pontoppidan's use of a minority in order to point up weaknesses of character in the majority was seen to be a device and not any religious commitment. By the same token that good Christians could take offense at parts of *Lykke-Per*, critics who themselves were Jews found nothing to object to, but whether the early declaration of, for example, Edvard Brandes, brother of Georg, that *Lykke-Per* was a masterpiece had any connection with his religious background and was not aesthetically and objectively motivated is a matter of conjecture.

The consensus of both the earlier critics and early readers was positive. The recognition that Pontoppidan had indeed written a Danish masterpiece spread until this concept became a tenet of literary history. As critic after critic turned his attention to the novel, it was sometimes to address one aspect and sometimes another, but always with the underlying assumption that the novel was worthy of the most serious consideration and that it was a work that profoundly influenced its readers. The attention paid to the actual construction and technique of the narrative was slight. Ethical substance blinded critics to possible flaws in the interrelationship of so many characters or the unlikelihood of some of the events and situations which Pontoppidan had invented. From the very first there was widespread praise for Pontoppidan as a stylist. He was seen to be a master of the Danish language and to write with classical simplicity and clarity. Pontoppidan's masterful use of the language together with the inherent social criticism in *Lykke-Per* were probably the reasons that moved the young Martin Andersen-Nexø, who later was to become Denmark's most famous Marxist, to dedicate his own first novel, *Pelle Erobreren* (*Pelle the Conqueror*) to Pontoppidan in 1906. While

Andersen-Nexø moved progressively to the left and finally became a leading apologist for the Soviet Union, Pontoppidan remained unchanged and nonpartisan, so that one could speak of a growing ideological gap between the two men, as similar as they were at the beginning of the century. This gave rise on Andersen-Nexø's part to a revised attitude toward *Lykke-Per*, so that by 1937 his overall view of the novel was a negative one: Pontoppidan, he now explained, shows the reader only how Per Sidenius comes to terms with himself, but Per has removed himself from society.[12] That is, in emphasizing the need for a life philosophy for the individual, Pontoppidan has failed to address himself to the vast problem of rebuilding society and inculcating the general public, or even the reading public, with progressive ideas. One cannot really quarrel with Andersen-Nexø's revised opinion of *Lykke-Per*, for it is quite true that Pontoppidan has not contributed to the discussion of a solution of those larger problems which beset society of the twentieth century. By implication, he held to the conviction that the betterment of society rests first on the betterment of the individual. Here was a difference in viewpoints that could not be reconciled. Whether the individual or society should first be reformed remains an unanswered question.

While the Marxist reservations failed to detract from the veneration in which Pontoppidan's novel had come to be held, there was something of a shock evoked when, in 1957, the professor of comparative literature in the University of Copenhagen, Paul V. Rubow, wrote a series of newspaper articles[13] about the important Danish literature of the late nineteenth century. With some malice aforethought, he entitled the articles "Herman Bang and his Contemporaries," thus giving to Bang a rank which many felt belonged to Pontoppidan. Rubow, removed by more than half a century from the completed *Lykke-Per*, applied the criteria of aesthetic criticism of which he was Danish champion and found Pontoppidan somewhat lacking. Pontoppidan, he pointed out convincingly, simply was not the artist Bang was, for all Pontoppidan's mastery of Danish. Bang was original and creative and wrote like nobody before him in world literature; Pontoppidan was a traditionalist who wrote like Meïr Goldschmidt and various other more nationally oriented

Danish authors. Rubow saw in Per Sidenius the average Dane—a characteristic which, to be sure, would have contributed to rather than detracted from the novel's popularity—but he pointed out that Per is not really the same person in the several parts of the novel. Rubow had the courage, or audacity, to doubt that the young Per Sidenius actually could develop in the way that Pontoppidan lets him in the novel. Rubow questions, moreover, that Per Sidenius's way to cognition has been a progression. Instead he implies that Per's philosophical insight and self-recognition, so striking at the end of the novel, suggests superimposition rather than organic development; that is to say, the interference of the omnipotent author rather than a psychologically grounded and understandable development.

Rubow's charges cannot be dismissed lightly. They are in fact, at least in part, irrefutable. Yes, Pontoppidan could have developed his story more carefully. He could have attempted a different kind of realism both in his descriptions and in his dialogue. He could have made Per psychologically more plausible. Yet all this smacks of gilding the lily. The novel's impact from the beginning and for three generations of readers has been unmistakable and quite as irrefutable as Rubow's most incisive arguments. We are today left with two conclusions which do not easily synthesize: that Pontoppidan's *Lykke-Per* has its flaws of organization and development, and that it has exerted an impact upon its readers which can be equated only with that of a work like Goethe's *Faust* or Ibsen's *Peer Gynt*, both of which are also technically flawed and contain major characters who must be the bane of a modern psychologist.

It should be borne in mind that *Lykke-Per* exists in three distinct versions and that there are additional editions containing minor, mostly orthographical variants. Even before the final volume of the original eight-volume set was published in 1904, Pontoppidan was planning a revised version of the novel, and he requested the final judgment of the entire novel be reserved until this revised version appeared in 1905. The second version, an edition in three volumes, is indeed different from the original, and it was set from a completely new manuscript from Pontoppidan's hand. Pontoppidan's canonical version of the novel is the fourth (not the third) edition, published in 1918. (The third edition contained a minimal number of textual changes.) All subsequent editions of the novel are based on the fourth; the orthographic changes which the later editions contain were not made by Pontoppidan, but by his publishers or editors.

The criticism of the novel that has been given here was made on the basis of the first edition in eight volumes, although today's reader will ordinarily have access to the fourth (or a subsequent) edition. In order to understand Pontoppidan in his own development and *Lykke-Per* in its genesis and in its interrelationship to Pontoppidan's other, earlier works, a focus upon the first edition seemed necessary. Moreover, the subsequent changes were not radical. Although style and organization of the novel improve in the second and fourth editions, the basic narrative and ethical substance of the novel are unchanged. For him who would understand Pontoppidan as a stylist and determine what seemed important to him as an imaginative writer with regard to diction and syntax, in particular, a detailed investigation of the changes which the text of the novel underwent is a desideratum. Unfortunately the time and effort needed for a thorough analysis of the changes seem sufficiently intimidating that the analysis has not yet been carried out, despite some preliminary attempts and the good intentions of various critics. We remember that Pontoppidan not only rewrote *Lykke-Per* but almost all his other works too, so that a conclusive study of Pontoppidan as a stylist, with an examination of all versions of all the works, may never be undertaken because of the enormity of the task.

CHAPTER 10

Case Histories

A new group, the last, of short novels or novellas that Pontoppidan wrote while and just after completing *Lykke-Per*, deal chiefly with marital affairs and with basic problems inherent to family life. They are, perhaps wilfully and conscientiously, not autobiographical and are not intended to complement or augment the *magnum opus*, *Lykke-Per*. Pontoppidan is now playing the observer and analyst. The search for a life philosophy, the kernel of *Lykke-Per*, does not inform these critical tales, only one of which is analogous to the larger novel. Nor is the concern with the time's injustices of a social or political nature, as had been the case in many of the earlier stories. In some ways they are preparatory to the quintuple *De Dødes Rige* (*The Realm of the Dead*) which began publication in 1912, for that work is to large extent concerned with the vagaries and complications of personal relationships.

Det ideale Hjem (*The Ideal Home*, 1900), the earliest of these new novels, is another forceful reminder that Pontoppidan was writing at the time of the great Scandinavian debate on sexual morality (in which the Norwegian writer Bjørnstjerne Bjørnson was the much disputed central figure) and of the protracted reaction to numerous (generally misunderstood) plays by Henrik Ibsen. Now deploring the wild oats of his youth, Bjørnson had become a leader of a coalition of elements: on the one hand, conservatives who championed "purity" among the young and, on the other, feminists who condemned the double standard. In the face of disputation, of heated tempers regarding women's rights, and of demands for a higher morality, Pontoppidan attempted to be a purveyor of fact through the medium of fiction. In a newspaper article which was to bring considerable vituperation upon his head, Pontoppidan made the observation that among the rural population on the island of Zealand, with which he was well acquainted, the incidence of illegitimacy was high, as was the percentage of pregnant brides. These observations, which could not be disputed statistically, were not welcome in most Danish homes. By many, Pontoppidan was felt to have offended Danish pride merely by bringing the matter up. Such aspects of life were, as Elias Bredsdorff has pointed out in his documentary study of "the great Nordic war" (i.e., the debate) about sexual morality toward the end of the nineteenth century, "something one does not talk about."[1]

Only if one sees Pontoppidan before the proper background and only if one at the same time realizes how strong feelings about sexual mores ran in the 1880s, one can understand, retrospectively, the ideas which pervade the earlier *Mimoser* and the later *Det ideale Hjem*. To a reader now, it seems apparent that Pontoppidan is criticizing those wives who look upon a husband's straying from the path of chastity as absolute and sufficient reason for the termination of a marriage. They are, in his opinion, "sensitive plants" indeed. By suggesting that their standards and demands are both unrealistic and unreasonable, Pontoppidan places himself with the radicals, although, curiously enough, *Mimoser* was not interpreted correctly by many early critics, who assumed that the two sisters had in Pontoppidan's opinion acted correctly in dismissing their husbands for brief marital infidelity.

Most peculiar, however, is *Det ideale Hjem,* which seems to make a case against marriage in general and certainly casts doubts on the establishment of marriage, its intrinsic values and demands. The situation which Pontoppidan describes is a special one and the proposal that his hero advances is only possible in the community which Pontoppidan has created for his characters. There is a serious flaw in the general argument insofar as the women are charged with the entire responsibility of caring for their offspring without husbands, but depending on brothers with sufficient time and interest to play the role of a father to the children engendered by the biological father, whose function is over at the conception of the child.

Unlike *Lykke-Per*, which Pontoppidan was completing at the same time he wrote *Det ideale Hjem*, the short novel is not

Case Histories

a reflection of the contemporary society or a story of a man seeking a life philosophy and trying to find himself. Dr. Malling, the leading character in *Det ideale Hjem* has a ready made, inflexible life philosophy and has some of the zeal of a reformer. There is perhaps a bit of malevolence in Pontoppidan's giving him the name Adam; we recall incidentally that another one of the short novels written six years before, and also dealing with marital problems was entitled *Den gamle Adam* (*Old Adam*). It is hard to know how seriously the reader should take the proposals that this new Adam makes, for his program of free love and the biological fraternal family is not something that Pontoppidan espoused in any of his other books, or in real life. There is, moreover, something of the extremist in Adam, who holds a doctorate in zoology but who, we learn at the beginning of the story, is a strict vegetarian. Adam and his sister Ingeborg have a very close relationship. They are the children of a broken home; they live with their mother, although both are up in their twenties; any they scarcely know their father. When Ingeborg finally marries a young and rather unsuccessful physician, Adam's life pattern is disturbed. He himself falls in love with the daughter of a Jutland clergyman (or at least the daughter of the clergyman's wife, since there is some question about the child's paternity). Despite the recent publication of his programmatic book attacking marriage (whence the title of the novel is derived), Adam marries his Jutland sweetheart. The marriage is short-lived and he leaves his wife in order to return to his sister, who has been divorced from her husband after leaving him, and her two children. That is to say, Adam is about to enter into the "ideal" arrangement which he has described in his book. No thought is given to the baby that his own wife will soon bear, and for whom no comparable familiar arrangement is available, since his wife is an only child.

The short novel *Borgmester Hoeck og Hustru* (*Mayor Hoeck and Wife*, 1905) accepts marriage as a norm but is one of Pontoppidan's several portrayals of a mésalliance. In the same way, as for example, *Nattevagt* a decade before, the novel ends with the death of the wife—unmotivated within the narrative. The shadow of death hovers over the entire narrative, for Mrs. Hoeck is ill from the beginning of the tale. The events that led up to the present situation of estrangement between her and her husband the mayor come out through conversations between her and her sister, who had herself contracted an ill-advised marriage with a German military officer whom she met during the German occupation of part of Denmark in 1864.

Although Mayor Hoeck had started on a brilliant career as a jurist in Copenhagen, he had inexplicably accepted the appointment as the mayor of a small town in Jutland in which his wife Anne-Marie, who came from a family in economic straits, had grown up. The tensions between Anne-Marie and her mother-in-law are the more striking since the mother-in-law is a born Sidenius. We recall that Per Sidenius, the hero of *Lykke-Per*, was, in Pontoppidan's eyes, born into a family representative of the stifling traditionalism and parochialism that could exist in Denmark. To the mayor, his wife's transgressions are primarily that she maintains some relationships with persons she has known in her youth, accepts gallant compliments from other men, and enjoys the erotic overtones in the attention she is shown by men when she is out in company. The tragic relationship between husband and wife is heightened when the mayor, in a grotesque overassessment of his own social status, insists that their daughter, their only child after the death of a son, be sent to boarding school because she has evinced too friendly an attitude toward the son of the town treasurer by accepting his gift of an apple. Mayor Hoeck is unwilling or unable to attempt a reconciliation with his dying wife, whose only pleasure in life now comprises the visits she receives from her hunchbacked physician and an unresponsive clergyman.

The third short novel, *Det store Spøgelse* (*The Great Apparition*, 1907) is a pathetic tale about an innocent girl's guilty conscience, a poignant example of puritanical ethics causing unnecessary tragedy. Returning home after an innocent tryst with her fiancé, the servant girl finds the window through which she had crawled to get out to meet her young man locked. Even before this discovery, which for her is no less than cataclysmic, she has heard a mysterious sound that frightened her. There is no obvious or explicable source for the sound. Pontoppidan subtly identifies it with the "ghost," the apparition, later in the story.

The sound is a figment of the girl's imagination, of her guilty conscience. She has been brought up very strictly and knows the vague but harsh judgments her employer has passed on loose women. In desperation, the girl roams the area, afraid to return to her place of work and ashamed to go home. The intensity of her shame and distress upsets her mental balance and, whether intentional or not, she finds her death in a nearby river. Too late, it is made clear that she would have met understanding from her employer and love from her family, had she but explained the situation, for they knew her to be a good and honest girl; they were, furthermore, not without understanding of the powerful natural forces within a human being.

Taken by itself, the tale can be viewed as a psychological study of an immature soul under stress. Within the context of the many other tales of country life which Pontoppidan wrote, *Det store Spøgelse* is part of the mosaic of contemporary Danish life. Pontoppidan designed it to express his indignation about deplorable social conditions, a prevailing lack of humaneness among human beings, and the tragic if unexpected effects of a severe, arbitrary, and indefensible ethic, often taken more seriously by the naive common folk than by those urbane arbiters of behavior responsible for its creation and dissemination.

Hans Kvast og Melusine (1907) is the longest of the short novels. It tells a story that to a considerable extent parallels the earlier *Lykke-Per*. The hero, or rather the central character of the book, refuses to face reality and has a high opinion of his own abilities. "Hans Kvast" is a Danish term equivalent to the German "Hans Wurst"—roughly the English Merry Andrew or Jack Pudding. He is a fool, a boaster, a ridiculous person. The "Hans Kvast" of Pontoppidan's novel is a musical genius named Hugo Martens. The "Melusine," in legend a fay or supernatural being—is in this case his long-suffering wife. With regard to the symbolic title, it is noteworthy that, in an early interview with a Copenhagen journalist after the revised edition of *Lykke-Per* (1905) had appeared, Pontoppidan said that the name "Lykke-Per" was arbitrary and that he just as well could have called his hero "Klod Hans" (literally "clumsy Jack," but for all practical purposes still another term for "Hans Kvast," "Hans Wurst," or "Jack Pudding").[2] In other words,

Pontoppidan himself indicated the parallelism in the two books and the moralizing intent that informed them both.

Hans Kvast og Melusine is, however, not a novel of development and it begins *in medias res*. We do learn something about the backgrounds of the major character and his wife, but only in retrospect. When the narrative begins, Hugo Martens has already acquired a reputation both as a composer and something of a critic, has been married for several years, and is the father of two children. His affectations of dress and action bring him some ephemeral attention, but he is really at odds with the everyday world because of a lack of inspiration. While his wife continues to believe in him, her own family scarcely approves of her union and doubts her husband's capacity either as a husband or an artist. Unpaid bills threaten the household constantly, and the consensus of other critics of music seems to be that the gilt has worn off Hugo Martens and that he is not fulfilling his earlier promise.

Living from hand to mouth, longing for renewed recognition, waiting impatiently for a new musical vein to open in his soul, beset by the petty cares of everyday life, and continually compromising himself, Hugo Martens seeks some relief from reality and the pressures he feels by putting a very small calibre pistol to his head in a hotel room. Ultimately, Martens's dramatic but half-hearted attempt at suicide brings about the success he long had sought in vain: a public collection for his benefit enables him to take a sea journey along the Norwegian coast. This in turn provides the inspiration he needed to awaken his creativity, but this creativity seems almost accidental. His deportment on shipboard is, however, no more admirable than before. He is brusque toward his loving wife, is attracted to a young German woman (to whom he nevertheless fails to respond in the right vein at the right time: even as a would-be adulterer he is unsuccessful), and continues to be filled with self-pity and self-admiration.

Curiously enough, the selfish, egotistical artist enjoys success at that point in his career when the reader takes leave of him. While his may be something of a hollow victory, Hugo Martens has with a new musical composition once more gained the popularity he craved. Unlike Per Sidenius, he has learned no lesson, has not been chastened by experience, and has not acquired a different and satisfying life philosophy. He becomes a sort of counterpart to Per Sidenius, since he succeeds despite his weaknesses and not by overcoming them.

As in a number of his stories and short novels, Pontoppidan is somewhat heavy-handed in his treatment of relations between man and wife and in his superimposition of drastic conclusions to the situations that he has created. In the short novel *Den kongelige Gæst* (*The Royal Guest,* 1908), however, he maintains a psychological delicacy which suggests a closer understanding of real life than the crasser and more dramatic situations that predominate in earlier works. The nucleus of the story is very simple. A rural physician, Dr. Højer, and his wife are disappointed to receive a message that the relatives whom they expect to visit them at Shrovetide are not coming. Shortly thereafter there is a knock at the door and a distinguished looking stranger enters after explaining that he had intended to visit the local clergyman but has not found him home. The stranger does not give his name but calls himself Prince Carnival, and starts to entertain the physician and his wife by playing the piano and conversing with them. He talks them into attiring themselves in formal clothes for the evening and decorates their living room with fruit and flowers that he has brought with him. They have an entertaining dinner and conversation; the stranger sings to them in several languages and his animation particularly engages the physician's wife. After having introduced merriment and adventure into the small west Jutland household, but also a modicum of suspicion and jealousy into the heart of the physician, the stranger leaves, only to create a new mystery. It seems that the clergyman knows no one who corresponds to the description of the stranger and there is no rational explanation why he came to the physician's home or indeed what he was doing in the area.

This single experience is both inexplicable and indelible for the physician and his wife, whose relations to one another never could be completely the same as before the visit of the stranger. At least in the wife there is always a residue of longing for adventure and relief from the monotonous existence of life in western Jutland. The events of the one evening serve as an essentially unwelcome reminder that life could be otherwise, that dreams can be fulfilled, and that sensuousness has its own virtue. Because of the erotic overtone that the doctor's wife sensed that remarkable evening, the effect upon her is the more lasting. Many years later she can gaze into the distance and envisage the fateful and stimulating evening and its associations with a different reality.

Pontoppidan now shows himself to be more subtle in his psychological depiction than he was earlier. He has seemingly become more aware of the importance and ramifications of personal relationships. He attends not to the development of a philosophy of life but to the dependence and effect of one person upon the other, the considerable effort and finesse required in daily life when an individual is a member of a family, has marital obligations, or bears responsibility toward one or more other human beings.

In these several approaches to an understanding of human life in everyday Western culture, the topical, the description of contemporary conditions or even of surrounding nature, become less important. Concomitantly, Pontoppidan's imaginative writing acquires a broader validity. Problems of human coexistence as well as the solutions of those problems transcend all discussions engendered by momentary political, economic, and social conditions.

CHAPTER 11
Reassessment

I *A Broader Canvas*

*D*E *Dødes rige* (*The Realm of the Dead,* 1912–16) was originally published in five volumes. The individual volumes had titles of their own and the collective title was not used until volume five—and then only in a colophon. Instead, the series was simply identified as "a narrative cycle."[1] This fact lends a more autonomous quality to the single volumes than if they had been parts of a larger work that possessed a monolithic character, suggested by an overall title, that clearly transcended the constituent parts. The term "cycle" also implies a certain collective nature of the compound narrative: there is not one single dominant character or even dominant couple, although Torben Dihmer and Jytte Abildgaard, with whom the reader becomes well acquainted from the beginning of the narrative cycle, provide a connecting link throughout. The first volume is entitled *Torben og Jytte,* the names of the two central figures of the story. In this volume it is uncertain in which direction Pontoppidan is moving. The nucleus of the action is an unstable relationship between Torben Dihmer, a young estate owner, and Jytte Abildgaard, the daughter of a deceased governmental minister. They are repeatedly drawn to one another; but because of Jytte's uncertainty vis-à-vis Torben, the relationship is still up in the air at the end of the volume. Interwoven with this basic love story are elements pertaining to the political situation in contemporary Denmark at the beginning of the twentieth century and also the story of a country clergyman who loses his parish after having been found guilty of breaking the sixth commandment.

As the story begins, young Torben Dihmer is suffering from a serious illness and has gone to his paternal estate, Favsingholm,

115

to die. He is visited by a professor of medicine named Asmus Hagen who makes a fresh diagnosis and prescribes a new medicine for Torben that ultimately effects a complete remission of the illness which (according to Professor Hagen's description of the medication) apparently is thyroid deficiency. Half the first volume is devoted to the experiences which Torben and Jytte have when they both are visiting a resort spa near Genoa in Italy. The descriptions of the adventures of the two young persons and the many people whom they meet and talk to in Italy seems rather drawn out. The action is slower and the motivations less convincing than in the other two of Pontoppidan's multi-volume novels. In particular, it is difficult to understand Jytte's psychology, her inability to comprehend her own feelings toward Torben, and her fear of speaking with him face to face about their relationship. The political unrest of contemporary Denmark, although only part of the background, is mentioned repeatedly, particularly by an agent of the conservative political party that wants to put up Torben as a candidate for election to the Danish parliament.

Not only do the two major characters have difficulty communicating with each other, but Torben is given to metaphorical speech which makes the other persons in the story somewhat impatient with him. At the end of volume one, Torben is convinced that Jytte will not have him and he makes the sudden decision to return to Denmark, apparently with the conviction that he now will participate actively in Danish politics.

The second volume of Pontoppidan's narrative cycle is entitled *Storeholt,* the name of the country estate in Jutland that belongs to John Hagen, the brother of the professor who had cured Torben Dihmer in volume one. If the reader expects simply a continuation of the story from the first volume in the sequence, he is surprised and possibly even confused to discover that the first fifty pages of the volume are devoted to the life story of Søren Madsen, the so-called "mad smith" in the village of Enslev in southern Jutland. These fifty pages are practically a short novel in themselves in much the same spirit as Pontoppidan's short novels from the 1880s through 1908. Within the framework of *De Dødes Rige,* however, the first section of volume two provides the familial background for

Reassessment

several characters in the story, notably Søren's son Tyge. The least wanted of the Madsen children, he was born with a club foot, but ultimately becomes a party leader, a minister in the Danish government, and one of the most influential politicians of the country. Like so many Danes, Tyge has taken a name other than the patronymic Madsen and calls himself Tyge Enslev, after the village of his birth. Three of Søren Madsen's grandchildren—Tyge Enslev's nephews—also play leading roles in volume two: John Hagen and the twin brothers Paul and Johannes Gaardbo, one of whom is a physician and the other a clergyman in the same district where Storeholt is located. Pontoppidan interweaves several narrative lines in the second volume. At first some of them seem to be autonomous but eventually they are seen all to be interrelated. The story of Jytte Abildgaard is continued, although we now hear of Torben Dihmer only as a background figure. Jytte and her mother visit Storeholt at a crucial time. Not only is there political tension engendered by a forthcoming election but also a visit of Uncle Tyge Enslev in an electioneering errand, a marital crisis between John Hagen and his ambitious wife (who is the daughter of a wealthy coffee merchant in Copenhagen), a financial crisis in the administration of the Hagen estate, and a growing disagreement between the twin brothers Gaardbo. Jytte Abildgaard remains an enigmatic figure, never at peace with herself and uncertain of her feelings toward several suitors. She and Pastor Gaardbo, who only recently had lost his fiancée through death, are attracted to one another, but his attempts to achieve a more intimate friendship with Jytte are unexpectedly rebuffed while Jytte's motivations remain a puzzle. Even the defrocked clergyman Mads Vestrup from volume one reappears at a political meeting where, over the strong objections of Pastor Gaardbo, he gives a lengthy and somewhat confused address.

The central figure of volume two is Enslev, now an old man, who senses power slipping from his hands and who is making an endeavor to bolster his own position vis-à-vis a former protégé who is now the prime minister. The local election takes an unexpected turn in that Enslev attacks political meddling by men of the church, striking a serious blow at his nephew Pastor Gaardbo. At the same time he advances the candidacy of the gauche and not completely honest John Hagen. The two men are ultimately put up as candidates for election to the Danish parliament and, at least in part because of Enslev's support, John Hagen is decisively elected, and none too soon. Storeholt is facing bankruptcy and John can hope for further support from his father-in-law only because of the prestige and power that the parliamentary mandate suggests. As in volume one, the heavy hand of the dead, or in the case of Enslev, the dying, is felt throughout the narrative; the characters cannot disengage themselves from their past nor from the domination of individuals who already have gone to their reward. The only real champion of progress is Professor Asmus Hagen, who brought back Torben Dihmer from the realm of the dead, but his is a minor role in a group of people who are not forward looking or, on the whole, socially conscious.

The title of the third volume of this series, *Toldere og Syndere* (1914), is a Biblical illusion and is best translated as *Publicans and Sinners* (the word "toldere" literally means those who level customs duties). Once more, Pontoppidan begins with an unexpected narrative element. The arrival of Mads Vestrup in Copenhagen is depicted in some detail. The defrocked clergyman has been brought to Copenhagen to be exploited by Enslev's newspaper in the hope that Vestrup will weaken the position of the established church in the popular consciousness, particularly because Dean Blomberg (whom the reader will remember from *Lykke-Per*) has effected Vestrup's removal from his parish and been appointed minister of culture in the government. This speculation is erroneous; Vestrup looks upon Copenhagen as a modern Sodom and Gommorah. Through public meetings he attempts to function as a revivalist clergyman, and he meets with some success.

There is a strong undercurrent furnished by the political tensions of the time with frequent reference to Enslev, whose grasp is slipping and whose newspaper is losing subscribers as a result of the inner party warfare in which Enslev is engaged, as well as the intolerance informing some of his speeches. John Hagen, elected as a supporter to Enslev, enjoys his new position as a member of the Danish parliament, but his success on this front was hard won. Economic necessity forced him to sell the Storeholt estate to his father-in-law, the coffee merchant Søholm, with whom he has at best an ambivalent relationship. When Hagen by chance discovers that his wife is carrying on an affair, as he has long suspected, he completely loses control of himself and must be removed by the police to a padded cell. His day of glory has been brief. It is apparent that Pastor Gaardbo, whom he had defeated in the parliamentary contest, will win the next election, since the incarcerated Hagen has to be replaced as member of parliament.

The volume contains several vignettes that seem almost anecdotal. There is a depiction of Enslev at home being tended by his mistress of many years; there is a gathering of Copenhagen artists who are bohemian to the point of caricature; and there is a picture of the coffee merchant esconced upon his new estate. Before a background of these various events one sees the thin thread of narrative regarding Jytte Abildgaard, who now becomes more and more attracted to the painter Karsten From, one of her previous suitors whom she had seemed earlier to reject decisively.

The several threads of the narrative continue to be interwoven in the fourth volume, entitled *Enslevs Død* (*Enslev's Death*, 1915). While the volume begins with a description of the several problems with which the brothers Gaardbo, physician and clergyman, are beset in Jutland, and their subsequent estrangement for both religious and political reasons, the major setting of the story soon becomes Copenhagen. Because he has been true to his convictions as a man of medicine and refused to be intimidated by the coffee merchant Søholm, Dr. Gaardbo has had to relinquish his practice in Jutland and now seeks to eke out a living in Copenhagen. His brother the pastor has to be in Copenhagen to attend the sessions of the Danish parliament to which he has been elected.

The off-again, on-again relationship between Jytte Abildgaard and the artist Karsten From ultimately leads to their engagement and marriage, to the distress of Jytte's mother and to the disappointment of Torben Dihmer, who returns to Denmark at this juncture. Considerable space is devoted to the activities of the defrocked clergyman Mads Vestrup, who had been brought to Copenhagen originally as a pawn of Enslev's newspaper with the unspoken intent of attempting to weaken the hegemony of the clergy, against which Enslev and his henchmen inveigh. Vestrup, who has become a religious revivalist and has acquired a following in the city, is won over to the clerical camp both through the mercy of the bishop of Copenhagen and through a generous offer of an appointment as a collaborator on the newly founded clerical newspaper whose first editor turns out to be no less a person than the long-time editor of Enslev's party newspaper.

The demise of the partisan newspaper is symptomatic of the lessening of Enslev's political power, but Enslev remains the major character in the background through the entire volume. Enslev's fate as a politician is sealed; at the end, the corps of the faithful is very small. Nevertheless, Enslev is able to attract both attention and admiration within and without parliament, and at his death, which follows shortly after an effort to topple the government has met crushing defeat, Enslev enjoys a state funeral, for the entire country recognizes his stature when viewed in historical perspective. Enslev is a representative of the realm of the dead.

Still another suggestion of death is given by Torben Dihmer, who has lost in love, relinquished his political ambitions, and ceased taking the miraculous medicine that Professor Hagen had prescribed and that had saved him from death at the beginning of the narrative. In his case there can only be one prognosis.

The final volume of the series carries the name of the estate: *Favsingholm* (1916). In it, Pontoppidan brings all the strands of his narrative to a conclusion. The development of each strand is reasonable enough judged by the events which have preceded, although they do not seem inevitable. At several places in the story the reader is aware of alternatives which might assure a different and happier conclusion for one or the other person. There is a noticeable repetition of ideas, and there is essentially nothing new introduced into the basic narrative. Pontoppidan depends to a considerable extent on intensification, exemplified by his frequent use of the comparative form of adjectives and adverbs in describing the actions of the main characters.

Reassessment 121

The union of Jytte and Karsten proves indeed to have been a mésalliance; Jytte returns to the home of her deceased mother after discovering, in her sixth month of pregnancy, that Karsten has taken a mistress. Torben Dihmer has returned to his estate Favsingholm to die an unnecessary death (since he will not continue the medication Professor Hagen has prescribed). The political struggles that gained dominance in the earlier volumes of the series are relegated to the background, while internal strife within the church suggests the continuing human inability to achieve a reasonable and ordered society. Of the remaining major characters, Mads Vestrup is the first to die; his demise does not seem particularly well motivated and merely emphasizes the fact that he is no longer useful to the two forces (the liberal political party and the pietistic wing of the church) that exploited him in turn for their purposes. Most of the other characters die in short order: the wholesale merchant Søholm, Torben Dihmer, and finally Jytte Abildgaard. The two brothers who so long have been antipodes remain: Paul and Johannes Gaardbo, the former, a representative of the rationalistic enlightenment, and the latter, a representative of the altruistic but self-deluding church militant. Their mutual distrust has lasted until the very end of the story, when Johannes, now disenchanted both with politics and organized religion, seeks out his brother, who, by wish of Torben Dihmer, is established at Favsingholm, to effect a reconciliation.

There is no doubt that the reader is meant to sympathize with Paul Gaardbo, the down-to-earth and sensible, although hot-tempered and hard-headed, physician, and his faithful wife Meta, who have suffered much primarily because the doctor has been unwilling to compromise himself. He has not acceded to the wish of many ignorant patients (including Søholm) to prescribe unnecessary medicines for them.

The virtue of Paul and Meta's way of life is recognized by Jytte on her deathbed when she charges Meta to bring up her newborn child. Pontoppidan's sympathies seem clearly enough stated in that Paul Gaardbo greets his brother, in the penultimate sentence of the novel, with the words, "Oh, Johannes! Then you have really returned from the Realm of the Dead!"[2] The reader must conclude that Paul Gaardbo's rationalism, his positive attitude toward life, and his love of children can assure an acceptable life and grant entrance, as it were, to the realm of the living. Indecision, the struggle for power, unwillingness to face reality, misguided religious zeal, a tendency to superstition, and the inability to be oneself are the characteristics of the many persons who have lived and lost in the course of the narrative. Only the person who is true to himself, cost what it may, and the person who through trial and error achieves self-cognition are, in the final analysis, to be respected as individuals with whom the reader would wish to identify.

Thus the message of *De Dødes Rige* is basically the same as in *Det forjættede Land* and *Lykke-Per*; it is ultimately the simple Socratic dictum: Know thyself. To achieve peace of mind the individual must seek and find a tenable philosophy of life. Such a philosophy is not simply given. Those who are born to a life close to the soil may be considered nearer to a healthy or ideal existence, while urbanism and sophistication, learning and wealth bear the seed of destruction and misfortune within them. The farther one is removed from the simple life that embraces only the basic elements of human existence, the more difficult it becomes to maintain a natural equilibrium, to avoid temptation and compromise, and to obey honestly the tenets of one's innermost philosophical or religious conviction, which might also be identified as Kant's categorical imperative.

Pontoppidan is nevertheless not agitating for a Rousseauistic doctrine that would advocate "back to the soil," nor does he suggest that it is possible to turn the development of society back upon itself. He depicted the futility of such a dream in *Det forjættede Land*, for Emanuel Hansted was more fool than wise man. Dr. Gaardbo, on the other hand, is more wise man than fool, although he too has at times been foolish. Dr. Gaardbo is, however, scarcely a main character of *De Dødes Rige* and thus is not comparable to Emanuel Hansted or Per Sidenius. This fact suggests a major difference between the two earlier novels and the five volumes that constitute *De Dødes Rige*. It is more nearly a "collective" novel without a hero and may be said to a greater degree than either *Det forjættede Land* and *Lykke-Per* to give a picture of the times.

Reassessment

II Reformational Theses

Halfway through the composition of *De Dødes Rige* that as a continuum exposes many determinative aspects of contemporary Danish society, Pontoppidan felt moved to attack what might have been considered the inviolate part of the Danish establishment: the state church. This attack, entitled *Kirken og dens Mænd* (*The Church and its Men*, 1914), was originally a lecture given in the Jutland city of Aalborg. Its thesis is simple. Pontoppidan believed that the 1100 clergymen of the state church had become mere functionaries and were not performing those duties with which they spiritually had been charged. Pontoppidan was not attacking the church per se; we should remember that he himself stayed within the church and was buried from the church. But he was deeply perturbed by the acquiescence of the men of the cloth to mere form, by their worldliness, and by their tacit assumption that they somehow were better than other men and should be above criticism. Here Pontoppidan was outspoken, but his convictions are in reality the same that led him to depict the series of clergymen in several of his works. One notes that there is scarcely a clergyman in Pontoppidan's oeuvre who arouses the reader's unlimited admiration. The sole cleric who comes close to it is the "Polar Bear" in the short novel by that name (*Isbjørnen, The Polar Bear*) from the year 1887, but he is too extravagant and too much of a caricature to be taken seriously.

Well over thirty years after Henrik Pontoppidan had left the manse and tried to distance himself from the ecclesiastical heritage, he is still taking the church and its servants seriously. Here too, he is a critic and a reformer. In retrospect he now understands his clergyman-father's dedication and earnestness, even though the puritanical ideals seemed psychologically indefensible from a modern and anthropocentric point of view. Pontoppidan had originally rejected the rigidity and inflexibility of conservative Lutheranism. He now objects to the impracticability and flabbiness of the state church, which seems to exist for its own sake rather than for the spiritual welfare of its communicants.

While it would be misleading to label Pontoppidan a crypto-

God-seeker, he has already shown himself to be in search of a belief or philosophy of life. While not all religion is a philosophy of life, a philosophy of life nevertheless can be called a religion. If the organized church is to be the principal instrument in supporting a religion of any kind, it had best focus on aiding in the achievement and practice of such a philosophy. The young Henrik Pontoppidan had not found success within the religious establishment; nor does his alter-ego Per Sidenius find it. Henrik came later to an understanding of his father's devotion to the church, as did Per. Henrik/Per nevertheless remained critical of the religious establishment. As we have seen, Pontoppidan time and again wrote about clergymen who were grotesque, ineffective, or fraudulent but, until 1914, always through the medium of imaginative literature. Finally, he felt impelled to articulate his censure. Those who did not, would not, or could not draw didactic conclusions from Pontoppidan's fictional characters could not escape the trenchant and even caustic observations in his lecture, of which there were two printings. He was again, or still, a castigator; but he was also still a patriot. The changes he intimated were desirable and necessary could only have given Danish society greater integrity.

CHAPTER 12

A Capstone

UNLIKE Pontoppidan's other longer works, the final novel, from the year 1927, is without an involvement either with clergymen or the church. The sole religious overtone of the book is contained in its title, *Mands Himmerig* (*Man's Heaven*), part of a Danish proverb to the effect that man's own will is his heaven. The levels and circles of society which dominated in the other works are here replaced by the small but influential body of journalists who control a national press. The novel does have allusions to the political scene—one might say necessarily—but the theme of women's liberation, as symbolized in the figure of the leading female character, Ragna Nordby, is quite as important as the tensions of domestic politics.

The events of the novel take place shortly before the outbreak of the First World War, and conclude when news of the Battle of the Marne reaches Copenhagen in 1914, as the major figure, the journalist Niels Thorsen, dies after a strenuous and fundamentally unsuccessful life, and as Ragna Nordby prepares to journey to the front as a war correspondent. There is in this situation of the male character a faint hint of parallelism with Jens Peter Jacobsen's earlier novel *Niels Lyhne* (1880; Eng. tr. 1919): the leading characters of both novels share a name; they both die in wartime; they both had unhappy domestic experiences; they both were nonbelievers to the end. There is, however, no reason to assume that Pontoppidan was conscious of the parallelism—which attests not literary dependency but simply a common human situation that both writers clothed in personae of their own creation. To no small extent, the two writers did share a time and a national culture. They were, to a certain degree, contemporaries touched by many of the same political and social currents, although Jacobsen met an early death of tuberculosis in 1885, five years after *Niels Lyhne* had appeared and four years after Pontoppidan had published his first book.

Mands Himmerig is farther removed from Pontoppidan's own world of experience than many, indeed most, of his other books. He is here writing more objectively as an observer and critic of an urban scene than in those novels for which he gained renown. He had, to be sure, functioned for several years as a journalistic writer, but his temporary involvement with the daily press did not resemble that of his character Niels Thorsen, who in much of the novel is involved in a power struggle for the editorship of one newspaper. Defeated in that bid for power, Thorsen defects to the political opposition in order to satisfy his own ambition. Nor was Pontoppidan's private life comparable with that of Niels Thorsen, a ruthless man unappreciative of his loving wife who, pregnant and in despair, finally takes her own life, presumably motivated by the unfounded suspicion that her husband is erotically interested in the emancipated journalist Ragna Nordby. Ragna Nordby has made an impression on Niels Thorsen, but as a Valkyrie rather than an embodiment of Eros. He has a vision of her on his deathbed: she sweeps down from snow-covered mountains on skis, with a rifle slung over her shoulder; she is his guardian spirit, a figure, not from the Christian pantheon, but from old Scandinavian mythology.

Mands Himmerig, then, is primarily the story of a defeat, but without the suggestion of philosophical redemption that concludes *Lykke-Per*. The novel is more nearly akin to the early work *Det forjættede Land* and the intermediate work *De Dødes Rige*. Superficially, this last novel seems rather far removed from the other novels, but it is in fact the extension of a dramatic-narrative sequence that Pontoppidan had created two decades before. The principal connecting link is Ragna Nordby, the one figure in *Mands Himmerig* who knows her own mind, and who fights for an ideal she has some hope of achieving. She had been the heroine of Pontoppidan's play *Asgaardsrejen* (*The Wild Huntsman*, 1906). The title of the play refers to commotion made by the old Scandinavian gods. There are also connections with other works by Pontoppidan. One of the characters in *Mands Himmerig* is the philosophical Dr. Vadum, the central figure in the short novel *Et Kærlighedseventyr* (*A Love Story*, 1918), and another the poet Klemens Junge from the first version of the same work.

Ragna in the play is the same libertarian woman of the later novel, merely somewhat younger. The situation is similar in the play and the novel. In both works there is an older liberal who has fought with his pen (and who identifies himself as a "soldier" in the struggles for human rights, just as Pontoppidan himself was to do in his autobiography thirty-five years later). In the spirit of Ibsen, the reader of the play sympathizes with the older writer who has been misunderstood by a hypocritical society on the one hand and a young woman who would be herself and burst the bonds of the petit bourgeois on the other. It is not difficult to make a case for a parallel situation between Otto Kall, the older champion of freedom, and Ibsen's Dr. Stockmann, and for that matter between his niece Ragna and Dr. Stockmann's daughter Petra.

Pontoppidan's play is a connecting link between the early works, such as *Isbjørnen* (1887) or *Nattevagten* (1894) and the final novel *Mands Himmerig*. This fact lends to the novel considerably more substance than might be attributed to it for itself, since it must be viewed as a part of a larger argument and not merely as a late and not particularly moving narrative. The second version of the play (1928) bears the subtitle "A Prelude," and refers directly to *Mands Himmerig*, as evinced by a statement found facing the last page of the play which advertises the novel as telling "inter alia about Ragna Nordby's later fate."[1] In rewritten form, the play has become more melodramatic. Ragna Nordby's mother is more nearly hysterical, and consequently is responsible for the tension between Ragna and her home since Ragna was misunderstood as a child.

The reception of the original version of the play when it was given on a Copenhagen stage ("Folketeatret") January 26, 1907 is not uninteresting: the public seemed to take sides in the theater and the reviews in the two leading and opposing newspapers differed markedly. The conservative *Berlingske Tidende*[2] dismissed the piece as an interim work by Pontoppidan and stated that the young man in the play who thought himself engaged to Ragna should consider himself fortunate that he did not have to take such an unbalanced wife. The liberal *Politiken*, speaking for Georg Brandes's camp, exuded considerable enthusiasm and welcomed Ragna to Copenhagen as an embryonic journalist.[3] Despite the nominal success of the opening night (when the theater was sold out) and the praise from *Politiken's* critic, *Asgaardsrejen* was soon withdrawn from the repertoire and has not been performed since. The dramatic nature of the story was not commensurate with the favorable partisan reception that the play received that opening night. The 1928 version has never been performed.

Both plays by Pontoppidan, *De vilde Fugle* (*The Wild Birds*, 1902) and *Asgaardsrejen* (1906), intrinsically unimportant as they are when compared with Pontoppidan's major novels and short stories, emphasize the intended inner unity of Pontoppidan's work. Ideas, persons, and situations reappear, to suggest that much of his production must be viewed as permutations. In light of this fact, the propensity for rewriting assumes new significance. Pontoppidan is not rewriting merely to improve diction or style (and as a matter of fact, it is often debatable whether the changes represent actual improvement), but rather to express the same ideas in a different way: to put the characters he has created in a slightly different light. They are variations on a theme, as it were, whether recast in different books or reformed in their own images in the same book.

Such recasting and rewriting without setting off on new tangents or introducing fundamentally different kinds of raw material is a further demonstration of the ethical-philosophical nature of Pontoppidan's oeuvre. While it would be an indefensible oversimplification to claim that Pontoppidan's message is uniform or that the individual works are repetitions of single motifs, they do have a common quality created from the basic convictions that pervade them. From start to finish, Pontoppidan is a liberal critic of the foibles of modern society, of the prevalence of social hypocrisy, and of the human weaknesses inherent in certain institutions, notably the Danish state church. Superimposed on these critical persuasions is the conviction of the need for a life philosophy, the need to find or be oneself, the central motif of the multi-volume works, particularly *Lykke-Per*.

A Capstone

Yet the ironic depiction of society and its weaknesses never ceases. For good reason, Pontoppidan is identified as a literary portraitist of Denmark between about 1880 and 1910, but the portrait is never a generic one. He writes not as an ethnologist or folklorist, nor is he a mere chronicler. If a historian, he is a critical historian who would arouse his readers. If he interposes the idyll into a description, it is only to effect a contrast or to destroy the idyll with slashing realism or cutting irony. One may wonder therefore that a recent young, left-wing critic has attempted to label Pontoppidan a reactionary, suggesting that Pontoppidan accepted the established order.[4] The state, social mores, the church, and even the politically motivated press, were all unacceptable to Pontoppidan as he found them. We recall the author's description of himself in the final volume of his autobiography: "A common soldier in mankind's eternal struggle for emancipation."[5]

The confusion regarding Pontoppidan's philosophical-social persuasion has probably been generated by his interest in Nietzsche who, rightly or wrongly, is often associated with the strong, antidemocratic, authoritarian current that has been the cause of such disaster in the twentieth century. In point of fact, Nietzsche was also dissatisfied with the established order. He was, moreover, a stimulating thinker. The concept "Übermensch" which he employed was not meant as a prototype of a modern militarist, either of fascist or national-socialistic persuasion. The identification of Nietzsche with the extreme political right is made by persons who have but a superficial acquaintance with his writings. Pontoppidan's acquaintance was not superficial. Actually, Pontoppidan's educible life philosophy is closer to Goethe's, as expressed in Goethe's life and in his *Faust;* development on the one hand of the individual ("die persönliche Bildung"), and on the other, of altruistic endeavor. Per Sidenius and Dr. Faust have not a few traits in common, although Per never achieves any practical humanitarian and altruistic goal as does Faust just before his death. To find themselves, both had to lose themselves. Yet they do not live in a vacuum. They are inevitably confronted by society as it exists and they must accept, reject, or try to reform it, with its restrictions, conditions, and assumptions.

CHAPTER 13

Reflections

BETWEEN 1933 and 1940 Pontoppidan published four small volumes of autobiography which covered approximately the first third of his life in some detail but which devoted few pages to the later years. Oddly enough, his compulsion to rewrite his works, a constant in his career as an author, extended even to the memoirs, and in 1943, at the age of 86, he published a fifth autobiographical volume that was not a continuation but a summary and revision of the first four. Not only does this fifth small volume, entitled *Undervejs til mig selv* (*Underway to myself*) condense the four previous volumes into one-third the space, but it shifts emphasis, in particular by the omission of some material but also, more strikingly, by factual changes. Some incidents are now sufficiently different to contradict the details or the chronology of certain events. As there is no diminution in the lucidity of presentation, this fact would seem to be an interesting bit of evidence about the changing past and the inability of the human mind to reconstruct historical evidence infallibly. One is reminded of the title of Goethe's autobiography: *Dichtung und Wahrheit*.

Since Pontoppidan did not write critical or philosophical essays in which he expounded his own convictions (with the exception of his separately published lecture on "The Church and its Men" from the year 1914), the autobiographical notations are the major source of first-hand evidence about Pontoppidan's life and opinions. Much of the time, the tone of the memoirs clearly echoes what the reader has been able to deduce from the imaginative works, but not always. Occasionally there are surprising discrepancies between the mood that pervades Pontoppidan's fiction and that of the late memoirs. There are, moreover, observations about writers and artists which could not be deduced from any of Pontoppidan's narrative. There is, finally, a store of anecdotes about his family life, some of his friends, and his travels that could not have been amalgamated into fiction, although the amount of information that Pontoppidan provides the reader about his private life really is minimal. He rarely provides the names of persons other than public figures (not even his two wives and his children are named!), and he seldom furnishes dates. There is something paradoxical about Pontoppidan as his own biographer: he is as intent on withholding information as communicating it. He is loathe to furnish details about any relationship or event that could be considered personal. He speaks to a public that he would keep at a distance. The memoirs, and particularly the final, revised volume, are nevertheless evidence that he felt compelled to write about his own life. Noteworthy is the fact that Pontoppidan's mastery of Danish syntax and diction and the clarity of his style were preserved to the end.

He who begins to read Pontoppidan's memoirs of his childhood and youth with the expectation of finding a clear-cut parallel between them and the first part of the novel *Lykke-Per,* which is regularly identified as semi-autobiographical, will be surprised, for Pontoppidan's own boyhood, or at least his recollection of it, shares only certain outward characteristics with the boyhood of Per Sidenius. The dominant mood of *Drengeaar* (*Boyhood Years*, 1933) is one of cheerful inquisitiveness. There is, to be sure, no attempt made at a systematic presentation of all of the young Pontoppidan's experiences. Instead, selected events are vividly and charmingly described—the early years at school, walking trips through the countryside, a first affair of the heart, the founding of a kind of literary society (of six members) at secondary school. Here and there, however, are more general remarks in which the older writer (Pontoppidan was seventy-six when the first volume of his memoirs was published) expresses his mature convictions openly. In particular, there is some criticism directed at the Catholic Church, ultimately engendered by the young Henrik's brief flirtation with the Church when he was about fifteen which had left considerable unpleasantness in its wake after it was discovered in Randers that the son of the local Lutheran clergyman was consorting with a Catholic priest.

The early memories also have a certain value, judged historically. The young Pontoppidan was an eyewitness to some events of significance in Danish history, notably the occupation of Jutland by German troops in 1864, when he was seven years old. He could also attest the impact of the news of N. F. S. Grundtvig's death, upon his father, among other people, in 1872. Other less significant but homely details give the reader an impression of the world in which Pontoppidan grew up, and suggest the difference in the quality of life in Denmark between the nineteenth and the twentieth centuries. In the second volume, *Hamskifte* (*Sloughing*, 1936), Pontoppidan writes also of his relationship to three of his brothers who were in Copenhagen at the same time as he. The picture is one of amity wthout any particular closeness, but with considerably more familial piety than his alter-ego Per Sidenius shows in *Lykke-Per*.

Of particular note are Pontoppidan's remarks about the *belles lettres* that seemed important in his early years, a time when there was no suggestion that he himself might develop into one of Denmark's most prominent imaginative writers. As a schoolboy he was most taken by Steen Steensen Blicher (1782–1848), and Adam Oehlenschläger (1779–1850), and Hans Christian Andersen, although he harbored reservations about Andersen's person. Blicher and Oehlenschläger had been contemporaries but were separated as the day from night with regard to their own ways of life and styles of writing. Blicher is the Danish writer who has had the greatest overall appeal and has maintained his popularity with the Danish public for well over a century. He was the poet of the heath and consequently something of a local celebrity in Jutland, and, in fact, had for a time lived in Randers. Adam Oehlenschläger had been the champion of a new, national, and historically oriented direction in literature during the early years of the nineteenth century and was as closely identified with Copenhagen as Blicher was with Jutland. Blicher was primarily a storyteller; Oehlenschläger primarily a dramatist. Danish and Norwegian drama, through the early work of Ibsen, clearly shows the impact of Oehlenschläger's pathetic, neoclassical style. It is perhaps well to point out here, to avoid any misinterpretation, that Hans Christian Andersen was not looked upon simply as a writer of children's stories in his own country, but was and is accepted in Denmark as a literary genius who worked in several genres, even though the well-known tales also occupy first place in Danish as well as foreign evaluation of his work.

The youthful Henrik Pontoppidan's literary inclinations were simply one with the times. The writers to whom he paid the most attention, also including the epic poet Christian Winther (1796–1876), would probably have been those that any young man or woman interested in contemporary literature admired around 1870.

In *Hamskifte*, Pontoppidan makes much of a friend and fellow student, who subsequently died young. Although Pontoppidan gave his name as Hansen-Schaffalitzky, no such person has been identified by Pontoppidan's Danish biographers, a fact which adds an air of mystery to the image of the self-possessed, ironic, and witty friend to whom Pontoppidan repeatedly indicates he was spiritually indebted. It was "Schaff" who directed the young Pontoppidan to the Russian writers, and especially Dostoevsky, that are mentioned in volume three of the memoirs, *Arv og Gæld* (*Inheritance and Debt*, 1938), as having made a particular impression upon him.

In *Arv og Gæld* he also discusses his somewhat delayed discovery of Georg Brandes, toward whom he had reservations similar to those he had earlier harbored toward Hans Christian Andersen, because of what he had heard of Andersen's personal idiosyncrasies. How ambivalent a relationship to Brandes Pontoppidan had is documented by an anecdote in which Pontoppidan tells of crossing Kattegat on a ferry with a garrulous Brandes whose egocentricity and need for an admiring audience unpleasantly affected Pontoppidan. Despite his literary productivity, Pontoppidan attempted only to establish a spiritual bond with his readers, and never sought the plaudits of the multitude by any kind of demagoguery, valuing privacy above popularity. Pontoppidan's caustic remarks a decade after the death of Brandes provide a contrast to the expressions of mutual admiration, reserved as they may be from Pontoppidan's side, contained in the correspondence between the two men, about which Elias Bredsdorff has written in detail.[1]

In this third volume of the memoirs, but also again in the

fifth, Pontoppidan made a point of objecting to the "ornamental word embroidery"[2] of his older contemporary Jens Peter Jacobsen,[3] whose international fame rests to a large extent upon his command of description, with an emphasis on adjectives describing color. This was not the first time that Pontoppidan had taken the painfully exact and detailed descriptions of Jacobsen amiss: the consensus of critics is that the figure of Enevoldsen in *Lykke-Per*, who is noted as spending a day forging a single sentence and ever seeking *le mot just*, is clearly meant as a caricature of Jacobsen. For the poet Holger Drachmann, who also appears in disguise in *Lykke-Per*, he seems to express a preference; Drachmann was an outspoken, virile, socially conscious, if also slightly unbalanced, lyric genius.

In the fourth volume of the memoirs, *Familieliv* (*Family Life*, 1940), Pontoppidan claims to have read relatively little until he established residence in rural Zealand for the second time after the birth of his second child with his second wife in 1896. His reading was unsystematic and included foreign as well as Danish writers. He mentions the two Norwegian contemporaries, Hans E. Kinck and Knut Hamsun, with respect and the former of these with particular admiration,[4] although Kinck is relatively unknown today compared to Hamsun.

Like Per Sidenius in *Lykke-Per*, Pontoppidan turned to philosophical and religious works to clarify his own ideas about the riddle of existence. Noteworthy is his expression of preference for the Old Testament to the New.[5] The image of a weak and suffering Christ who at the same time could be a Saviour he ultimately found unacceptable. Of particular note was his interest in Friedrich Nietzsche,[6] whose collected works Pontoppidan seems to have read one winter, instigated by the debate about Nietzsche carried on by Georg Brandes and the Danish philosopher Harald Høffding. Pontoppidan recognized in Nietzsche "really a new, creative spirit, a spirit with the wings of a stormy petrel compared, for example, with Kierkegaard, whose criticism of the time and its men always struck me as quite narrow-minded."[7]

Not surprising is the fact that there is an undercurrent of religious thought, or perhaps more precisely of assuming a stance toward organized religion in the memoirs, for this had characterized almost all of Pontoppidan's earlier works. Pontoppidan declares himself to be an out-and-out rationalist with implicit faith in the power of human reason and with an aversion to all religious ceremony that smacks of Rome. Odd, however, is his formulation that there were moments "when I considered myself fortunate to have descended from an old family of Lutheran clergymen."[8]

In *Arv og Gæld* Pontoppidan speaks freely about his stance vis-à-vis the church and agrees with the conclusion drawn by Per Sidenius in *Lykke-Per* that "neither solace nor help was to be found any place outside myself."[9] Divine services he had come to look upon "as a pitiful substitute for real, awesome reverence for life itself and its dark origins."[10] And in *Familieliv* we can find the nearest thing to what might be called Pontoppidan's creed and confession of faith: "Is it not on the whole one of our most unfortunate delusions that we in our conscience—that attic full of all kinds of old, hidden superstitions and long superseded prejudices—that we in the spectral voice from that sepulchre possess a divine guide through life's labyrinth, a guide in whom we can put greater trust than in the supreme human good: our reason."[11]

Time and again Pontoppidan's relationship to organized religion caused him anguish because it placed him in a position where he necessarily had to make a judgment that was counter to the opinions and desires of some members of his family. A passage in *Arv og Gæld*, for example, tells of his distress when he is unable to support his brother Morten's efforts to collect funds in order to build a church adjacent to the brother's folk-high-school where Henrik Pontoppidan taught for several years. Here too, Pontoppidan speaks of his own religious conviction:

I still was unable to understand those people who could be comforted and elevated by ecclesiastical ceremonies, but it was neither because of animosity nor jealousy that I was reticent about helping build new refuges for the old superstitions. That was simply my make-up. And I didn't wish to be any different. Why should I? Despite my rather restless path through life, I could myself experience moments when I felt as if I were in a sanctuary—grand, festive moments when the dreariness of everyday suddenly was filled with light as if from radiant candles and hymnic notes filled my breast. Moments, when the spectres and trolls of my old melancholy that were still lying in wait for me, sank deep into the earth.[12]

The conclusion of the summary, fifth volume of memoirs gives evidence of Pontoppidan's indomitable spirit and his belief in the ultimate victory of rational thought. There was reason for the seriousness of his final words to his readers, for he was writing during World War II and the German occupation of Denmark. After describing himself as a onetime soldier in the battle for the liberation of the human race he concludes his autobiography, and thus his published work, with the sentence, "There must come a time when reason again rules the world and creates an existence one need not be ashamed of."[13]

CHAPTER 14

Conclusion

I *Pontoppidan's Stature*

DESPITE Pontoppidan's sharing the Nobel Prize for literature in 1917, he has only here and there been acknowledged outside Scandinavia as a figure of world stature in imaginative literature. There are translations of several of his works into German and into Hungarian, but very few into French and English. The dearth of translations means that there can be no widespread acquaintance with his works among speakers of English and French. There probably has been a minimal circle of acquaintance with Pontoppidan outside Denmark, despite the fact that in Denmark itself his books continue to appear in new editions. Intelligent readers who do not know Danish or Swedish or German or Russian or Polish or Dutch or Rumanian or Finnish (the languages in which *Lykke-Per* has appeared), that is, very many members of the republic of letters, cannot even have the chance of reading Pontoppidan's most important work.[1] The more the pity: he is a living part of Danish literature. He has a place in the consciousness of every Danish reader, for he is an integral part of the Danish literary tradition. Extracts from his works appear as schoolbooks or in readers. Students of cultural and social history can and do draw upon Pontoppidan as a source. Students of style find in him an inexhaustible source of information, examples, and inspiration.

In view of the fact that Pontoppidan did get the Nobel Prize and several of his works have been translated into various languages, it is a bit difficult to understand how he remains practically unknown in the English-speaking world. The first two volumes of his trilogy *Det forjættede Land* were translated into English by Mrs. E. V. Lucas in 1896; but the final volume was not translated. Very few of his stories have been published in English translation. Some critics attempt to explain this dearth of Pontoppidan in English by pointing out that many of his stories are localized in Denmark and that therefore readers in the English-speaking world would miss many of the associations which Danish readers usually make. This argument is not very convincing, however, since his books have been successfully translated into other languages and since writers in other languages who are more provincial than Pontoppidan have appeared in English translation. That his *magnum opus*, *Lykke Per*, has not appeared in English can probably be ascribed to the fact that it is very lengthy. Economic considerations have weighed more heavily than aesthetic in discussing the desirability of publishing a translation of the work.

In short, Pontoppidan remains something of a phenomenon in world literature. He is a major and lasting figure within the *belles lettres* of his own country, has received much recognition abroad, and has even been widely read in translation, while nevertheless remaining pretty much an unknown quantity for a large and important segment of the world of literature: readers of English.

Worth quoting here are some words that Thomas Mann wrote about Pontoppidan on the occasion of the Danish novelist's seventieth birthday in 1927 and which were published in Danish translation in the Copenhagen daily *Politiken*: "The author of *Lykke-Per* is a born epic poet and as a critic of life and society enjoys European stature. A true conservative, who in a breathless world has preserved the grand style in the novel. A true revolutionary, who in his prose above all has kept its power to pass judgments in view. With the winning and delightful severity that is the secret of art, he has judged the times and, like the true poet which he is, pointed toward a purer humanity."[2]

II A *Summation*

In retrospect one can conveniently divide Pontoppidan's work into four periods. One might speak of major strands of narrative art in the same sense that Knut Ahnlund did in his Swedish dissertation on Pontoppidan in 1956,[3] although the present review of Pontoppidan's oeuvre does not make the same substantial divisions or temporal subdivisions as does Ahnlund.

In the first instance, Pontoppidan was one with his time in reacting against social injustice. He represented that direction of *belles lettres* in the 1880s labelled "naturalistic," which saw in daily life, even if it be humdrum existence, subject matter quite as worthy of treatment as was adventure or romance. The naturalists argued that it is less of an effort to portray the unusual and the exciting or to produce a variant of the *Wunschbild*—the dream of an exciting life and successful achievement, an escape from reality—than comprehensibly to depict what can be seen every day. We have observed that Pontoppidan did not write about the indigent but hard-working peasant merely because that was an unworked narrative vein any more than he wanted simply to suggest a rural idyll or to admire the honesty and uprightness of the exploited tiller of the soil. He wrote both because he perceived what hitherto had been overlooked and because he hoped to arouse his readers to a new cognition of social conditions. He was motivated both by indignation and the desire through the printed word to help the less fortunate. At the same time he was writing, new problems of urbanization and industrialization were making themselves felt elsewhere, but he was independent of the advocates of political reform. He might have heard of Marx, but he never read Marx. He was clearly an independent observer seeking a philosophical position of his own.

The social criticism was not confined to a note of distress evoked by the oppression of small folk in the countryside. Pontoppidan took a broader view. In particular, the position of the church was brought into question and the irritating self-satisfaction of the Grundtvigian movement was made apparent. There was, further, an awareness of the contrast between town and country, between the governors and the governed, although Pontoppidan levelled no partisan charges and made no specific suggestions for change. He espoused no party platform.

A skepticism toward organized religion is noticeable from the start in Pontoppidan's writing. This characteristic is easily explained. Athough Pontoppidan was the son of a conservative Lutheran clergyman, his modern orientation and interest in the natural sciences and engineering did not permit him to accept without question the traditional faith. As a consequence, the entire metaphysical structure of Lutheran Christianity threatened to come tumbling down, leaving the individual in a state of chaos. The skeptical, naturalistic social awareness of the young Pontoppidan moved him into a position where he himself had to seek to reestablish a belief; he must create his own metaphysical pattern. At this juncture he wrote his critical, social novel *Det forjættede Land* (*The Promised Land*). But the promised land was reached neither by the leading character of the book nor by its author. Indeed, *The Promised Land* is philosophically a monument to failure, to the inability of the old order to adjust to new times or to accept a new reality. It is no accident that the central character of the novel is a clergyman, and a fool in more than one sense of the word: he is naive, he is ignorant, he is selfish.

Coexistent with Pontoppidan's social indignation and his skepticism toward the traditional state and church was the second strand: his patriotism, his predilection for life in Denmark. At every point in his career as a writer, he evinced appreciation for the Danish landscape. Even when he used descriptions of nature for an ironic purpose (as so frequently was the case), he nevertheless preserved an intimate relationship and a receptive attitude toward nature in his homeland. Pontoppidan travelled and lived abroad a great deal, particularly in Germany, Italy, and Norway, but when he left Denmark, it was not to flee the country or to seek some better spot on earth, some ideal land which possessed those virtues which Denmark lacked. Experiences abroad were interesting and enlightening, but Denmark remained for him the norm of existence.

Pontoppidan was sensitive to all aspects of landscape and seascape. With an unsurpassed freshness, he could describe them both in their infinite variations. Early criticism of Pontoppidan regularly identified him as a naturalist.[4] On the basis of his transmutation of landscapes into words, he might well be classified as an impressionist, but such a label would have to be burdened with so many reservations that it really would lose all validity. The young Pontoppidan could just as easily be labelled a "nature writer" since he was so often concerned with the natural scene and addressed himself to an accurate portrayal of what he observed. No wonder, then, that he was asked to contribute chapters on various parts of Denmark to a monumental topographical work of the day. Just as Pontoppidan could illustrate the social conduct of Danish peasants naturalistically, so too was he able to look upon the Danish landscape with fresh eyes. Moreover, he was able to combine the depiction of social conditions and the depiction of landscape so that the one suggested the other, as is so strikingly the case at the beginning of the story "Gallows Hill at Ilum" in the collection *Skyer*.

In the course of the 1890s the third strand of his oeuvre becomes prominent: the need to establish a life philosophy. As this demand became more insistent for Pontoppidan, he subjugated his tendency to description and observation of the surroundings to philosophical reflection and to the need of the individual to find himself and to assess his relationships with other human beings. The sublimated account of this struggle constitutes Pontoppidan's *magnum opus*, *Lykke-Per* (1894–1903), in which autobiographical elements predominate at the beginning of the narrative, so convincingly that the reader finds the story less of a construct than might otherwise be the case. Pontoppidan was exposing a sensitive nerve of his own experience, although there can be no equation of Per Sidenius ("Lykke Per") with Pontoppidan himself. The social order is no longer being questioned so sharply, but attention is called to the individual's right to affect the lives of other human beings. The sins of pride, arrogance, and ambition are flayed so that the reader recognizes in Per Sidenius his own failings. Per's discovery of himself is convoluted and Pontoppidan does not endeavor to address himself solely to the ethical point of his tale. He views the hero in a historical context: he has been born into a certain society; his efforts to remold society according to his self-centered ideas and needs are unsuccessful; and he withdraws from society in order to find himself. He has unhappy experiences in the basic situations of the human being: as a child vis-à-vis his parents, brothers, and sisters; as a schoolchild and student; as a lover, husband, and father. He was not only a failure in all these situations; he failed to satisfy his own ambitions and to achieve worldly success. Only when he discovered that the ambitions themselves were defective and that worldly success ultimately failed to provide satisfaction, was he in a position to take on a new role in society, and at this juncture, Pontoppidan let "Lykke-Per" die. His creator could, however, apply some of his acquired wisdom and the life philosophy that experience, reflection, and cognition had given him. Addressing himself to the basic questions of individual human life, he could now view situations through the lens of his newly gained perception. Incidentally, the Faustian message of altruistic endeavor is educible from *Lykke-Per,* although Per himself did not realize it. That was left to his abandoned fiancée, Jakobè Salomon, who was something of an outsider in Danish society because of her Jewish heritage. Per Sidenius finally found himself, but it cost him a life to do so and he served no purpose outside himself. Jakobè Salomon was herself, and devoted all her energies to making for a better society.

Some of the situations and ideas of *Lykke-Per* appear in other narratives by Pontoppidan, but the core of his novel is the questioning of certain conditions that occur in Western civilization, in particular the relationship between man and woman, especially within a marriage. To be sure, this element is not peculiar to Henrik Pontoppidan; it was a part of the dialectic and ratiocination of the time. From the 1870s on, the questions of the ideal marriage, of women's rights, and of sexual mores had been under increasingly intense discussion, in particular the matter of sexual morality evoked a kind of drawn battle in Scandinavia. In his books, although less in public debate, Pontoppidan took his stand among the radical forces that questioned traditional marriage. Pontoppidan even suggested a rather grotesque alternative to marriage (in *Det ideale Hjem— The Ideal Home,* 1900). He went along with those who abjured hypocrisy with regard to sexual morality and who excused, if they did not advocate, free love. Several pathetic life stories are found in Pontoppidan's short novels that touch upon issues that were troubling both Scandinavian and the larger European society. The complex of questions that can be identified with this aspect of Pontoppidan's career is less easy to confine temporally. One of the short novels written in 1894 (*Den gamle Adam*—*The Old Adam*) is in part the story of a marriage broken up by a man's attraction to a goose of a young woman, but the possible rights of passion and free love are still the subject of the last of the "short novels," *Et Kærlighedseventyr* (*A Love Story*, 1918). And the possibility of a satisfactory solution was less likely in the first novel dealing with the rights of Eros than in the last, twenty-five years later.

The fourth and final strand of Pontoppidan's creativity is represented by the five-volume novel *De Dødes Rige* (*The Realm of the Dead*, 1912–16) in which all of the motifs and ideas that had been touched upon hitherto once more found expression. On the one hand, it is a picture of the times, a chronicle of the early years of the twentieth century, but on the other, it is a warning to Pontoppidan's countrymen about the forces which threatened to constrict, change, or destroy their world. The narrative does not concentrate upon an individual; to a certain extent it may be called a collective novel (a term of more recent vintage). The social situation being depicted is more important than the fate of any individual. There is, however, much interrelationship of the characters, as much as in a drama by Ibsen, where characters are skilfully and artfully, but also artificially, interdependent. Their interdependence in Pontoppidan's novel is sufficiently complex and well-grounded that the reader does not find it forced and unacceptable. Pontoppidan delineates multiple levels of society: none is without its problems. The older Pontoppidan viewed society as a whole, but it was Danish and not just any Western society which he analyzed in exemplary fashion.

There was no new phase generated in Pontoppidan's work after World War I. A return to his biographical point of origin was gradual, and perhaps inevitable in an author who was still writing as a septuagenarian and octogenarian. Between 1938 and 1943 he produced memoirs which, without being particularly revelatory, tell something about his earlier years and corroborate various theses regarding the genesis of some of his work. Neither at the beginning nor at the end of his career was Pontoppidan satisfied with the state of the world, but, writing in 1943 a few months before his death at the age of eighty-six, he was not dissatisfied with himself for what he had tried to accomplish. He knew that he had done his share toward the emancipation of the human spirit.

Notes and References

Chapter One

1. See F. J. Billeskov Jansen, *Ludvig Holberg* (Boston: Twayne's World Author Series, No. 321, 1975).
2. See Kenneth H. Ober, *Meïr Goldschmidt* (Boston: TWAS 414, 1976) 146 pp.
3. See Bertil Nolin, *Georg Brandes* (Boston: TWAS 390, 1976).

Chapter Two

1. In a review of *Sandinge Menighed* in the journal *Ude og Hjemme* VI (1883), p. 462.

Chapter Three

1. The play was given at the Dagmar Theater in the 1913–14 season only. The film was made in 1920 by the Skandia Film Corporation of Stockholm.

Chapter Four

1. Described by Elias Bredsdorff in *Den Store Nordiske Krig om seksualmoralen* (Copenhagen: Gyldendal, 1973).

Chapter Five

1. *Skyer* (Copenhagen: Gyldendal, 1890), p. 11.
2. *Ibid.*
3. *Københavns Børstidende*, 5, 6, 7, 8 December 1889.
4. *Københavns Børstidende*, 5 December 1889.

Chapter Six

1. In *Danmark*, ed. Martinus Galschiøt, vol. I (Copenhagen: P. G. Philipsen, 1887), p. 250.
2. *En Vinterrejse* (Copenhagen: Gyldendal, 1920), p. 62.
3. *Ibid.*, p. 36.

Chapter Seven

1. *Muld* (Copenhagen: 1891), p. 3.
2. *Ibid.*
3. *Ibid.*, p. 6.
4. *Ibid.*
5. *Ibid.*
6. *Ibid.*, p. 7.
7. *Ibid.*, p. 9.
8. *Ibid.*, p. 3.
9. *Det forjættede Land* (Copenhagen: 1892), p. 88.
10. *Ibid.*, p. 3.
11. *Ibid.*, p. 4.
12. *Ibid.*, p. 3.
13. *Emmanuel or Children of the Soil; The Promised Land*, both London, J. M. Dent, 1896.
14. *Dommens Dag* (Copenhagen: 1896), p. 233.
15. *Ibid.*, p. 255–56.

Chapter Eight

1. *Den gamle Adam* (Copenhagen: 1894), p. 142.
2. *Ibid.*, p. 134.

Chapter Nine

1. *Lykke-Per i det Fremmede* (Copenhagen: 1899), p. 69.
2. In *Drengeaar* (1933), the first volume of his memoirs, Pontoppidan mentions an estate by this name in Jutland (p. 65). It is difficult to determine whether he meant to communicate any idea with the name (which can mean "beloved island"). "Kjær" is not an uncommon family name in Denmark.
3. *Lykke-Per. Hans Rejse til Amerika* (Copenhagen: 1903), p. 162.
4. *Lykke-Per. Hans sidste Kamp* (Copenhagen: 1904), p. 270.
5. See Nolin, *Georg Brandes*, pp. 156 ff.
6. Reprinted in Danish translation in *Omkring Lykke-Per*, ed. Knut Ahnlund (Copenhagen: 1971), pp. 138 ff., 173.
7. There are translations into Dutch, Finnish, German, Hungarian, Norwegian, Polish, Rumanian, Russian, and Swedish, and a partial translation into French.
8. See the bibliography in *Omkring Lykke-Per*, and the entries under Henrik Pontoppidan in *Dansk skønlitterært forfatterleksikon 1900–1950* vol. III (Copenhagen: Grønholt Pedersen, 1964).

Notes and References

9. Jørgen Bukdahl, *Spejling og realitet* (Copenhagen: Gyldendal, 1962), pp. 206–15.
10. Notably Vilhelm Andersen, Edvard Brandes, Sven Lange, Poul Levin, and Niels Møller.
11. "Henrik Pontoppidan," in the Norwegian periodical *For Kirke og Kultur* XI (1904), pp. 292–94 (rep. in *Omkring Lykke-Per*, pp. 40–45).
12. In the Communist newspaper *Arbejderbladet*, 24 July 1937 (rep. in *Omkring Lykke-Per*, pp. 195–98).
13. In *Berlingske Aftenavis*, 23 July 1957 (rep. in *Omkring Lykke-Per*, pp. 265–66).

Chapter Ten

1. Bredsdorff, pp. 11 ff.
2. Interview with C. C. Clausen, in the Danish weekly *Hver 8. Dag*, 10 September 1905 (rep. in *Omkring Lykke-Per*, p. 57).

Chapter Eleven

1. The title page of each volume in the series bears the superscript, "En Fortælling-Kres" ("A Narrative Cycle").
2. *Favsingholm* (Copenhagen: 1916), p. 222.

Chapter Twelve

1. In its turn the novel has a statement facing the last page of text identifying the previously published play *Asgaardsrej*en as "a prelude" to the novel.
2. *Berlingske Tidende*, 27 January 1907.
3. *Politiken*, 27 January 1907.
4. Jørgen Holmgaard, *Dødens Gilding* (Copenhagen: Munksgaard, 1971).
5. *Undervejs til mig selv* (Copenhagen: 1943), p. 194.

Chapter Thirteen

1. Elias Bredsdorff, *Henrik Pontoppidan og Georg Brandes. En kritisk undersøgelse af Henrik Pontoppidans forhold til Georg Brandes og Brandes-linjen i dansk åndsliv* (Copenhagen: 1964).
2. *Arv og Gæld* (Copenhagen: 1938), p. 43.
3. Jens Peter Jacobsen completed only two novels, *Marie Grubbe* (1876), set in the seventeenth century, and *Niels Lyhne* (1880;

Eng. tr. by Hanna Astrup Larsen. New York: The American-Scandinavian Foundation, 1919; reissued by Twayne in 1967) set in the nineteenth century. Adjectives pertaining to color are particularly striking in *Marie Grubbe* (Eng. tr. by Hanna Astrup Larsen. New York: The American-Scandinavian Foundation, 1917; reissued by Twayne in 1975).
4. *Familjeliv* (Copenhagen: 1940), p. 92.
5. *Ibid.*, p. 16.
6. *Ibid.*, pp. 79–84.
7. *Ibid.*, p. 80.
8. *Ibid.*, p. 66.
9. *Arv og Gæld*, p. 78.
10. *Ibid.*, p. 79.
11. *Familjeliv*, p. 102.
12. *Ibid.*, p. 112.
13. *Undervejs til mig selv*, p. 194.

Chapter Fourteen

1. There is only a partial translation of *Lykke-Per* into French.
2. Rep. in *Omkring Lykke-Per*, p. 173.
3. Knut Ahnlund, *Henrik Pontoppidan. Fem huvudlinjer i författarskapet* (Stockholm: 1956).
4. The early critical consensus toward Pontoppidan's works is demonstrable by an examination of random reviews from the first twenty-five years of his career as a writer. In *Ude og Hjemme* for 17 June 1883, Otto Borchsenius characterized Pontoppidan's depictions as "grey on grey" but nevertheless "fresh, new, and original." An anonymous review of *Dommens Dag* in *Ungt Blod*, Nr. 3 for 1895 (p. 177) found Pontoppidan the "incomparable delineator of popular social, political, and religious movements of the time." Reflecting on Pontoppidan's first works, Sven Lange stressed the "small, clear pictures from the lives of the humblest" (*Det ny Aarhundrede* IV [1906], February–March, p. 474), while Vilhelm Østergaard spoke of "sketches that are realistic and living images of Danish popular life and culture" (*Illustreret Tidende*, 28 October 1906, p. 44). The less kindly disposed Christian Gulmann called Pontoppidan the "purest Danish realist" but added enigmatically that his art was "wingless romanticism" (*Ord och Bild* XVI [1907], pp. 102–103).

Selected Bibliography

PRIMARY SOURCES

1. Books

Stækkede Vinger. Copenhagen: Andr. Schous Forlag, 1881.
Sandinge Menighed. En Fortælling. Copenhagen: Andr. Schous Forlag, 1883.
Landsbybilleder. Copenhagen: Gyldendalske Boghandels Forlag, 1883.
Ung Elskov. Idyl. Copenhagen: Gyldendalske Boghandels Forlag, 1885.
Mimoser. Et Familieliv. Copenhagen: Gyldendalske Boghandels Forlag, 1886.
Fra Hytterne. Nye Landsbybilleder. Copenhagen: Gyldendalske Boghandels Forlag, 1887.
Spøgelser. En Historie. Copenhagen: Gyldendalske Boghandels Forlag, 1888.
Skyer. Skildringer fra Provisoriernes Dage. Copenhagen: Gyldendalske Boghandels Forlag, 1890.
Reisebilder aus Dänemark. Copenhagen: Andr. Fred. Höst & Sön, 1890.
Natur. To smaa Romaner. Copenhagen: Det Schubotheske Forlag, 1890.
Krøniker. Copenhagen: P. G. Philipsens Forlag, 1890.
Muld. Et Tidsbillede. Copenhagen: P. G. Philipsens Forlag, 1891.
Det forjættede Land. Et Tidsbillede. Copenhagen: P. G. Philipsens Forlag, 1892.
Minder. Copenhagen: P. G. Philipsens Forlag, 1893.
Nattevagt. Copenhagen: P. G. Philipsens Forlag, 1894.
Den gamle Adam. Skildring fra Alfarvej. Copenhagen: P. G. Philipsens Forlag, 1894.
Dommens Dag. Et Tidsbillede. Copenhagen: P. G. Philipsens Forlag, 1895.
Højsang. Skildring fra Alfarvej. Copenhagen: Det Schubotheske Forlag, 1896.
Kirkeskuden. En Fortælling. Anden Udgave. Copenhagen: Det Schubotheske Forlag, 1897. (Revised version of "Kirkeskuden" from *Stækkede Vinger*, 1881).

HENRIK PONTOPPIDAN

Lykke–Per. Hans Ungdom. Copenhagen: Det Nordiske Forlag, 1898.
Lykke–Per finder Skatten. Copenhagen: Det Nordiske Forlag, 1898.
Det forjættede Land. Copenhagen: Det Nordiske Forlag, 1898. (Collected, revised edition of *Muld*, 1891, *Det forjættede Land*, 1892, and *Dommens Dag*, 1895).
Lykke–Per. Hans Kærlighed. Copenhagen: Det Nordiske Forlag, 1899.
Lykke–Per i det Fremmede. Copenhagen: Det Nordiske Forlag, 1899.
Fortællinger I–II. Copenhagen: Det Nordiske Forlag, 1899. (Contains *Fra Hytterne, Isbjørnen, Krøniker, Minder, Skyer, Den gamle Adam,* all revised).
Lille Rødhætte. Et Portræt. Copenhagen: Det Nordiske Forlag, 1900.
Det ideale Hjem. Aarhus: Jydsk Forlags-Forretning, 1900.
Lykke–Per. Hans store Værk. Copenhagen: Det Nordiske Forlag, 1901.
Lykke–Per og hans Kæreste. Copenhagen: Det Nordiske Forlag, 1902.
De vilde Fugle. Et Skuespil. Copenhagen: Det Nordiske Forlag. Ernst Bojesen, 1902.
Lykke-Per. Hans Rejse til Amerika. Copenhagen: Det Nordiske Forlag, 1903.
Lykke–Per. Hans sidste Kamp. Copenhagen & Christiania: Gyldendalske Boghandel. Nordisk Forlag, 1904.
Borgmester Hoeck og Hustru. Et Dobbeltportræt. Copenhagen & Christiania: Gyldendalske Boghandel. Nordisk Forlag, 1905.
Lykke–Per. Anden Udgave I–III. Copenhagen & Christiania: Gyldendalske Boghandel. Nordisk Forlag, 1905.
Asgaardsrejen. Et Skuespil. Copenhagen: Det Schubotheske Forlag, 1906.
Ung Elskov. Blade af en Mindekrans. Copenhagen: Det Schubotheske Forlag, 1906. (Revised ed. of *Ung Elskov*, 1885).
Det store Spøgelse. Copenhagen: Det Schubotheske Forlag, 1907.
Hans Kvast og Melusine. Copenhagen: Det Schubotheske Forlag, 1907.
Den kongelige Gæst. Copenhagen: Det Schubotheske Forlag, 1908.
Torben og Jytte (at head of page: *En Fortælling–Kres*). Copenhagen & Christiania: Gyldendalske Boghandel. Nordisk Forlag, 1912.
Storeholt (at head of page: *En Fortælling–Kres*). Copenhagen & Christiania, 1913.
Toldere og Syndere (at head of page: *En Fortælling–Kres*). Copenhagen & Christiania: Gyldendalske Boghandel. Nordisk Forlag, 1914.
Kirken og dens Mænd. Et Foredrag. Copenhagen & Christiania: Gyldendalske Boghandel. Nordisk Forlag, 1914.

Selected Bibliography 151

Enslevs Død (at head of page: *En Fortælling–Kres*). Copenhagen & Christiania: Gyldendalske Boghandel. Nordisk Forlag, 1915.
Favsingholm (at head of page: *En Fortælling–Kres*). Copenhagen & Christiania: Gyldendalske Boghandel. Nordisk Forlag, 1916. (Identified in colophon as final volume of series *De Dødes Rige*).
De Dødes Rige. Anden Udgave I–II. Copenhagen & Christiania: Gyldendalske Boghandel, 1917.
Lykke–Per. Fjerde Udgave. Copenhagen & Christiania: Gyldendalske Boghandel. Nordisk Forlag, 1918.
Et Kærlighedseventyr. Copenhagen & Christiania: Gyldendalske Boghandel. Nordisk Forlag, 1918.
En Vinterrejse. Nogle Dagbogsblade. Copenhagen & Christiania: Gyldendalske Boghandel. Nordisk Forlag, 1920.
Noveller og Skitser. Et Udvalg. I–II. Copenhagen & Christiania: Gyldendalske Boghandel. Nordisk Forlag, 1922. (Contains *Sandinge Menighed, Ung Elskov, Fra Hytterne, Isbjørnen, Krøniker, Vildt, Skyer, Den gamle Adam, Thora van Deken, Borgmester Hoeck og Hustru, Den kongelige Gæst*, all somewhat revised).
Mands Himmerig. Copenhagen: Gyldendalske Boghandel, 1927.
Asgaardsrejen. Et Forspil. Anden Udgave. Copenhagen: Gyldendalske Boghandel. Nordisk Forlag, 1928.
Noveller og Skitser. Et Udvalg. Copenhagen: Gyldendalske Boghandel. Nordisk Forlag, 1930. (Volume III of *Noveller og Skitser*. Contains *Det ideale Hjem, Hans Kvast og Melusine, En Vinterrejse, Rabbinerens Datter, Et Kærlighedseventyr, Rejsen gennem Livet*).
Drengeaar. Copenhagen: Gyldendalske Boghandel. Nordisk Forlag, 1933.
Hamskifte. Copenhagen: Gyldendalske Boghandel. Nordisk Forlag, 1936.
Arv og Gæld. Copenhagen: Gyldendalske Boghandel. Nordisk Forlag, 1938. (Colophon identifies this volume as one of a series: *Undervejs til mig selv*).
Familieliv. Copenhagen: Gyldendalske Boghandel. Nordisk Forlag, 1940.
Undervejs til mig selv. Et Tilbageblik. Ny Udgave. Copenhagen: Gyldendalske Boghandel. Nordisk Forlag, 1943.

2. Translations into English

Mimoser: *The Apothecary's Daughters*. Translated by G. Nielsen. London: Trübner & Co., 1890.

Muld: Emanuel or Children of the Soil. Translated by Mrs. Edgar Lucas. London: J. M. Dent & Co., Aldine House, 1896.
Det forjættede Land: The Promised Land. Translated by Mrs. Edgar Lucas. London: J. M. Dent & Co., 1896.
"En Fiskerrede": "A Fisher Nest." Translated by Julianne Sarauw. *The American–Scandinavian Review* XV (1927), 476–86.
"Ørneflugt": "Eagle's Flight." Translated by Lida Siboni Hanson. *The American–Scandinavian Review* XVII (1929), 556–58.
"Ilum Galgebakke": "Gallows Hill at Ilum." Translated by David Stoner. *Anthology of Danish Literature; Bilingual Edition.* Ed. F. J. Billeskov Jansen and P. M. Mitchell. Carbondale: Southern Illinois University Press, 1971 (paperback ed., 1973), pp. 333–59.
Den kongelige Gæst: "The Royal Guest." *The Royal Guest and Other Classical Danish Narrative.* Ed. P. M. Mitchell and Kenneth H. Ober. Chicago: University of Chicago Press, 1977, pp. 143–93.

SECONDARY SOURCES

1. Bibliographies

ANDERSEN, POUL CARIT, *Henrik Pontoppidan. En Biografi og Bibliografi.* Copenhagen Levin & Munksgaard, 1934.
DAHL, SVEND et al., *Dansk skønlitterært forfatterleksikon 1900–1950.* Copenhagen: Grønholt Pedersens Forlag, 1964, III, pp. 112–22.

2. Selected Books

AHNLUND, KNUT, *Henrik Pontoppidan. Fem huvudlinjer i författarskapet.* Stockholm: Norstedt, 1956. An attempt to delineate the major currents in Pontoppidan's oeuvre, by a perceptive Swedish critic.
————. ed. *Omkring Lykke–Per.* Copenhagen: Hans Reitzel, 1971. An annotated collection of letters, reviews, and excerpts from critical studies having to do with Pontoppidan's magnum opus. With a bibliography. An indispensable reference tool.
ANDERSEN, POUL CARIT, *Digteren og Mennesket. Fem essays om Henrik Pontoppidan.* On Pontoppidan's relations to his childhood's city of Horsens, to his publishers, and to journalism, as well as on the author's own interest in Pontoppidan and collection of books by Pontoppidan.
ANDERSEN, VILHELM, *Henrik Pontoppidan. Et nydansk Forfatterskab.* Copenhagen: Gyldendalske Boghandel. Nordisk Forlag, 1917. The first attempt to view Pontoppidan's works as a whole and the origin of the concept of Pontoppidan's essential ambivalence.

Selected Bibliography 153

BILLESKOV JANSEN, F. J., *Henrik Pontoppidan. Ledetråd for Læsere.* Copenhagen: Nordisk Bogforlag, 1977. A critical guide to all of Pontoppidan's works by the former Professor of Danish literature in the University of Copenhagen.

BREDSDORFF, ELIAS, *Henrik Pontoppidan og Georg Brandes. En kritisk undersøgelse af Henrik Pontoppidans forhold til Georg Brandes og Brandes-linjen i dansk åndsliv.* Copenhagen: Gyldendal, 1964. A detailed study of the relations between the critic Brandes and the writer Pontoppidan which concludes that the two men had more in common and shared more mutual respect than ordinarily has been assumed.

―――. *Henrik Pontoppidan og Georg Brandes. En redegørelse for brevvekslingen.* Copenhagen: Gyldendal, 1964. Brandes' letters to Pontoppidan with paraphrases and résumés of Pontoppidan's letters to Brandes. This arrangement was made necessary because of the provision in Pontoppidan's will that his letters should not be printed.

HOLMSGAARD, JØRGEN. *Dødens Gilding. En analyse af Henrik Pontoppidans 'Lykke–Per'.* Copenhagen: Munksgaard, 1971. An attempt to criticize Pontoppidan's major novel by means of A. J. Greimas' "structural semantics." Retells the plot of *Lykke–Per* and concludes that it is politically reactionary.

JEPPESEN, BENT HAUGAARD, *Henrik Pontoppidans samfundskritik. Studier over den sociale debat i forfatterskabet 1881–1927.* (Studier fra Sprog- og Oldtidsforskning, 250.) Copenhagen: G. E. C. Gads Forlag, 1962. Pontoppidan's works examined as evidence of social criticism and as a reflection of the concern with social issues at the time.

JEPPESEN, NIELS, *Samtaler med Henrik Pontoppidan.* Copenhagen: Rosenkilde & Bagger, 1951. Reports of conversations the author had with Pontoppidan.

JOLIVET, ALFRED, *Les romans de Henrik Pontoppidan. Cinquante années de vie danoise.* Paris: Bibliothèque nordique, 1960. A sober review of Pontoppidan's major works (not only the longer novels) as historical documents; Pontoppidan as a champion of justice and integrity.

SKJERBÆK, THORKILD, *Kunst og Budskab. Studier i Henrik Pontoppidans Forfatterskab.* Copenhagen: Gyldendal, 1970. In part a contribution to the complicated textual history of Pontoppidan's works; in part a review of other critical works about Pontoppidan. Discusses the interrelationship of Pontoppidan's many books and the genesis of the autobiography.

THOMSEN, EJNAR, ed. *Henrik Pontoppidan til Minde.* Copenhagen:

Gyldendal, 1944. A memorial volume with contributions by several hands. The most important item is the editor's review of Pontoppidan's life and works, supported by pertinent quotations.

THOMSEN, KARL V., *Hold galden flydende. Tanker og tendenser i Henrik Pontoppidans forfatterskab.* Aarhus: Søren Lund, 1957. Personal reflections about works by Pontoppidan, with a social-critical bias.

WOEL, CAI M., *Henrik Pontoppidan* I–II. Copenhagen: Ejnar Munksgaards Forlag, 1945. Plot summaries and brief assessments of each of Pontoppidan's books, chronologically ordered, with bibliographical notations. (The original issue of Woel's study was recalled because it reprinted Pontoppidan's poetry which was unauthorized).

3. Selected Articles

BRANDES, GEORG, "Henrik Pontoppidan," in his *Samlede Skrifter,* vol. III, 2nd edition. Copenhagen: Gyldendal, 1919, pp. 310–24.

BREDSDORFF, ELIAS, "Henrik Pontoppidans Verhältnis zum radikalen Denken." *Nordeuropa,* 3 (1969), 125–42.

———. "Da Henrik Pontoppidan blev strøget på f..nansloven." *Fund og Forskning,* XXI (1974), 137–64.

BRIX, HANS, "Henrik Pontoppidan: Det forjættede Land," in his *Gudernes Tungemaal.* Copenhagen: Gyldendal, 1911, pp. 156–64.

———, "Henrik Pontoppidan," in his *Danmarks Digtere,* 3rd edition. Copenhagen: Aschehoug, 1955, pp. 446–56.

BUKDAHL, JØRGEN, "Idealet og Virkeliggørelsen," in his *Dansk national Kunst.* Copenhagen: Aschehoug, 1929, pp. 163–220.

———, "Don Quijotes skygge," in his *Spejling og realitet.* Copenhagen: Gyldendal, 1962, pp. 206–15.

EKMAN, ERNST, "Henrik Pontoppidan as a Critic of Modern Danish Society." *Scandinavian Studies,* XXIX (1957), 170–83.

FRANDSEN, ERNST, *Aargangen der maatte snuble i Starten.* Copenhagen: Gyldendal, 1943, pp. 60–76.

GEISMAR, OSCAR, "Henrik Pontoppidan." *For Kirke og Kultur,* XI (1904), 278–95.

———, "Henrik Pontoppidan." *The American–Scandinavian Review,* XXI (1933), 7–12.

GRODAL, TORBEN KROGH, " 'Nattevagt' og den socialhistoriske analyse." *Poetik,* VI/1 (1974), 69–88.

HESSELAA, BIRGITTE, "At sætte problemer under debat." *Kritik,* 19 (1971), 44–63.

HOLMGAARD, JØRGEN, "Ørnens flugt fra plankeverket." *Analyser af*

Selected Bibliography 155

dansk kortprosa. Ed. Jørgen Dines Johansen. Copenhagen: Borgen, 1971, I, pp. 283–96.

JONES, W. GLYN, "Henrik Pontoppidan 1857–1943." *Modern Language Review,* LII (1957), 376–83.

——, "Henrik Pontoppidan, the Church and Christianity after 1900." *Scandinavian Studies,* XXX (1958), 191–97.

——, " 'Det forjættede Land' and 'Fremskridt' as Social Novels." *Scandinavian Studies,* XXXVII (1965), 77–90.

KAARSHOLM, PREBEN, "Pontoppidans 'Nattevagt.' " *Poetik,* VI/1 (1974), 50–68.

KRISTENSEN, SVEN MØLLER, "Lykke–Per," in his *Digtning og livssyn.* Copenhagen: Gyldendal, 1963, pp. 57–91.

KRISTENSEN, TOM, "Henrik Pontoppidan og Ungdommen," in his *Mellem Krigene.* Copenhagen: Gyldendal, 1946, pp. 112–15.

LARSEN, HANNA ASTRUP, "Pontoppidan of Denmark." *The American-Scandinavian Review,* XXXI (1943), 231–39.

LAURIDSEN, HELGA VANG, "Lykke–Per." *Danske Samfundsromaner.* Copenhagen: J. H. Schultz, 1946, pp. 21–33.

LAURIDSEN, OLAF, "Henrik Pontoppidans Stilling til Radikalismen." *Edda,* XXXVIII (1938), 165–210.

MADSEN, BØRGE GEDSØ, "Henrik Pontoppidan's Emanuel Hansted and Per Sidenius." *Scandinavian Studies. Essays Presented to Henry Goddard Leach.* Ed. Carl Bayerschmidt and Erik Friis. Seattle: University of Washington Press, 1965, pp. 227–35.

MOESTRUP, JØRGEN, "Lykke–Per og Nietzsche." *Omkring Lykke–Per.* Ed. Knut Ahnlund. Copenhagen: Borgen, 1971, pp. 292–322.

MORTENSEN, KLAUS P., "Det provisoriske land." *Kritik,* 41 (1977), 58–93.

NIELSEN, FREDERIK, " 'Ørneflugt' læst igen," in his *Digter og læser.* Copenhagen: Gyldendal, 1961, pp. 148–63.

ROBERTSON, J. G., "Henrik Pontoppidan," in his *Essays and Addresses on Literature.* London: George Routledge & Sons, 1935, pp. 245–54.

RUBOW, PAUL V., "Henrik Pontoppidan," in his *Herman Bang og flere kritiske Studier.* Copenhagen: Gyldendal, 1958, pp. 72–78.

SKOU-HANSEN, TAGE, "Fornægteren." *Heretica,* V (1953), 384–401.

SCHYBERG, FREDERIK, "Henrik Pontoppidan," in his *Digteren, Elskeren og den Afsindige.* Copenhagen: Thaning & Appel, 1947, pp. 86–96.

THOMSEN, EJNAR, "Henrik Pontoppidan," in Ejnar Thomsen, *Skribenter og Salmister.* Ed. Frederik Nielsen. Copenhagen: E. Wangels Forlag, 1957, pp. 24–46.

Index

Adam Homo (Paludan-Müller), 86
Ahnlund, Knut, 102, 138
Andersen, Hans Christian, 19–20, 22, 84, 132–33
Andersen, Vilhelm, 147n9–10
Andersen-Nexø, Martin, 42, 103–104

Bang, Herman, 13, 50, 66, 104
Bauditz, Sophus, 56
Bergsøe, Vilhelm, 56
Bergstrøm, Hjalmar, 36
Berlingske Tidende, 127
Bjørnson, Bjørnstjerne, 24, 40, 58, 107
Blicher, Steen Steensen, 19–20, 22, 38, 80, 132
Borchsenius, Otto, 25, 34, 148n14–4
Brandes, Edvard, 16, 56, 103
Brandes, Georg, 15–16, 22–23, 79, 89, 96, 100–101, 128, 133–34
Bredsdorff, Elias, 108, 133
Bukdahl, Jørgen, 101

Caesar, 87, 93
Christian IV, 55
Clausen, C. C., 147n10–2

Danmark (M. Galschiøt), 56
Darwin, Charles, 22
Dichtung und Wahrheit (Goethe), 130
Dostoevsky, Feodor, 15, 133
Drachmann, Holger, 15, 56, 134

Estrup, J. B. S., 46
Ewald, Johannes, 19

Faust (Goethe), 105, 129
Feilberg, H. F., 56

Feuerbach, Ludwig, 23
Fielding, Henry, 100

Galschiøt, Martinus, 56
Geismar, Otto, 102
Gjellerup, Karl, 13, 56
Goethe, J. W. von, 84, 100, 105, 129–30
Goldschmidt, Meir, 20–22, 57, 104
Goncourt, Edmond & Jules, 21
Grundtvig, N. F. S., 15, 19, 30–31, 62, 67, 132
Gulmann, Christian, 148n14–4

Hamsun, Knut, 134
Hansen-Schaffalitzsky, 133
Hegel, Frederik V., 35
Høffding, Harald, 15
Holberg, Ludvig, 19

Ibsen, Henrik, 19, 24, 53, 65, 105, 107, 127, 132, 143

Jacobsen, Jens Peter, 22, 31, 125, 134, 148n13–3
Jøde, En (Goldschmidt), 21
Jørgensen, Johannes, 56

Kierkegaard, Søren, 15, 19
Kinck, Hans E., 134
Københavns Børstidende, 48
Kristensen, Evald Tang, 56

Lange, Sven, 147n9–10, 148n14–4
Levin, Poul, 147n9–10
Lucas, Mrs. E. V., 69, 137
Lukács, Georg, 101

Mann, Thomas, 101, 138

Index

Marie Grubbe (Jacobsen), 148n13–3
Marx, Karl, 23, 139
Mill, John Stuart, 23
Møller, Niels, 147n9–10
Niels Lyhne (Jacobsen), 125–26
Nielsen, Zacharias, 56
Nietzsche, Friedrich, 15, 102, 129, 134
Oehlenschläger, Adam, 19, 132
Østergaard, Vilhelm, 148n14–4
Omkring Lykke-Per (Ahnlund), 102
Paludan-Müller, Frederik, 86
Peer Gynt (Ibsen), 105
Pelle Erobreren (Andersen-Nexø), 103
Politiken, 128, 138
Pontoppidan, Dines, 14, 16–17, (132)
Pontoppidan, Erik, 17
Pontoppidan, Henrik:
WORKS:
"Arv," 35
Arv og Gæld, 133, 135–36
Asgaardsrejen, 81, 126–28, 147-n12–1
"Bonde, En," 44
Borgmester Hoeck og Hustru, 109–10
Dødes Rige, De, 59, 107, 115–23, 126, 143
Dommens Dag, 70–72
Drengeaar, 131
"Efter Ballet," 28
"Endeligt, Et," 25–28
Enslevs Død, 119–20
Familieliv, 134–35
Favsingholm, 120–22
"Fiskerrede, En," 37
"første Gendarme, Den," 50–51
forjættede Land, Det, 30, 61–74, 78, 122, 126, 137, 140
Fra Hytterne, 41–44, 56–57
gamle Adam, Den, 57–58, 79–80, 109, 143

"Grundskud, Et," 43–44
Hamskifte, 14, 132–33
Hans Kvast og Melusine, 111–13
"Hans og Trine," 41
Højsang, 80–81
ideale Hjem, Det, 107–109, 142
"Ilum Galgebakke," 40, 46–52, 67, 79, 141
Isbjørnen, 40, 123, 127
Kærlighedseventyr, Et, 127, 143
"Kærlighedshistorie, En," 36–37
Kirken og dens Mænd, 123–24, 130
"Kirkeskuden," 28–29
"Knokkelmanden," 42
kongelige Gæst, Den, 113
Krøniker, 82
Landsbybilleder, 35–38, 44
Lille Rødhætte, 35–36, 145n3–1
Lykke-Per, 23, 29, 52–53, 83–106, 107–108, 110–11, 122, 134, 137, 141–42
Mands Himmerig, 125–27
Mimoser, 39–40, 108
Minder, 76
Muld, 61–67, 70
"Naadsensbrød," 41–42
Nattevagt, 78–79, 109, 127
Natur, 44
"Ørneflugt," 82
"Offer, Et," 50
Reisebilder aus Dänemark, 54–58, 76
Sandinge Menighed, 29–34, 35, 72
Skyer, 40, 42, 46–53, 141
Spøgelser, 44–45
Stækkede Vinger, 25–29
store Spøgelse, Det, 110–11
Storeholt, 116–18
"Tête à tête," 28
Thora van Deken, 36
"To Gange mødt," 50
"To Venner," 50
Toldere og Syndere, 118–19
Torben og Jytte, 115–16
Undervejs til mig selv, 130, (136)
Ung Elskov, 37–38

vilde Fugle, De, 80, 128
"Vildt," 44
"Vinterbillede, Et," 36
Vinterrejse, En, 58–60
Pontoppidan, Knud, 16
Pontoppidan, Morten, 16, 34

Rubow, Paul V., 104–105

St. Beuve, C.-A., 23
Schandorph, Sophus, 15, 21, 56
Schiller, Friedrich, 45
Schou, Andreas, 25
Skram, Amalie, 15

Skram, Erik, 15
Strauss, David Friedrich, 23
Strindberg, August, 19

Taine, Hippolyte, 23
Tom Jones (Fielding), 100

Ude og Hjemme, 25, 148n14–4
Ungt Blod, 148n14–4

Wilhelm Meister (Goethe), 84, 100
Winther, Christian, 133

Zola, Emile, 21